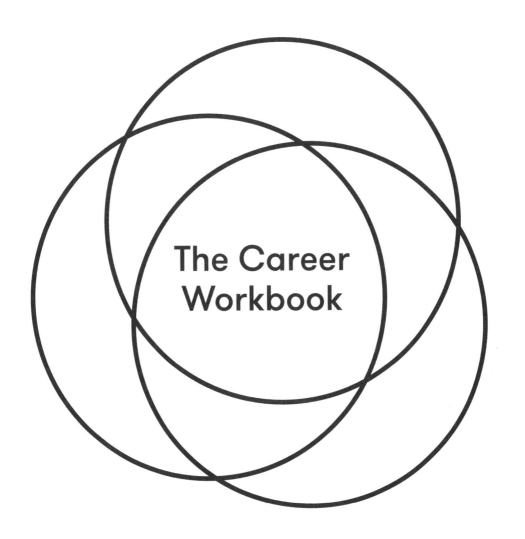

The Career Workbook

Fulfilment at work

Published in 2023 by The School of Life
930 High Road, London, N12 9RT
First published in the USA in 2023

Designed and typeset by Ryan Bartaby
Printed in China by Leo Paper Group

A proportion of this book has appeared online at:
www.theschooloflife.com/articles

The School of Life publishes a range of books on
essential topics in psychological and emotional
life, including relationships, parenting, friendship,
careers and fulfilment. The aim is always to help
us to understand ourselves better – and thereby to
grow calmer, less confused and more purposeful.
Discover our full range of titles, including books
for children, here:
www.theschooloflife.com/books

The School of Life also offers a comprehensive
therapy service, which complements, and draws
upon, our published works:
www.theschooloflife.com/therapy

www.theschooloflife.com

ISBN 978-1-915087-05-8

10 9 8 7 6 5 4 3 2

Introduction

Work is an immense part of existence: cumulatively we put more time and effort into it than anything else and it's come to hold a central place in our identity. Our society is obsessed with career success, but privately we often suffer from a powerful, nagging sense of being in the wrong job; we're depressed at the prospect of another week, another year of the same. Our work might not sound pointless or stupid to other people, but inwardly we feel we're wasting our lives.

The distress is plain enough; it comes out in moments of panic and gloom. But unfortunately knowing that we're deeply frustrated isn't the same as identifying a better direction: the mind registers the problem but doesn't create solutions.

That's what this workbook is for. Left to our own devices, we shy away from asking the pointed, tricky questions that could help us arrive at better answers. Instead of getting moody and distracted, as we understandably tend to do, this workbook holds us to working out – and actually writing down – what we think and feel on the wide range of topics that are relevant to improving our working lives.

Through forty-five essays and exercises, we will engage in a patient, structured way with who we are – and who we might become – in the world of work. Broadly, there are two overarching themes of investigation: what are the obstacles to us having a better experience of work and how, positively, can we come to know our true potential?

Obstacles

- We don't easily see the extent to which our thinking about work and our prospects is hemmed in by external psychological forces: our relationship to the expectations (or lack of them) of family and friends, as well as the broad cultural picture of status, respectability and success. These forces may have little connection to our intimate needs but can dominate our view of what is possible. And, ironically, it can be hard for us to detect their influence on us. They don't announce themselves as impositions but get inside our heads as voices telling us what's necessary. But with the right questions we can start to recognise them for what they are.

- To make a change is, necessarily, to take a risk, and we may be stymied by our fear of failure and rejection. Where are these fears coming from and why do they have such a powerful grip on our imaginations?
- Do we talk ourselves into soul-destroying pragmatism? In the short term there will almost inevitably be a case for sticking with the painful current situation. Why do we discount the larger expanse of life? Money can be the thorniest of issues because it feels like an absolute demand and yet – ultimately – it always has a hidden psychological dimension.

Knowing our true potential

- We've come (sadly) to disassociate pleasure from work, but identifying what we like doing is, in fact, a crucial guide to what we're good at.
- What's our ideal picture of work? We hold back, perhaps, because it feels like asking too much; it's mere fantasy. But our ideal hopes contain coded clues to the environments in which we could really thrive.
- Envy of others' careers feels embarrassing, but the right questions help us mine our envy to discover our own – perhaps more viable – desires.

A good career isn't one free of demands and troubles; it's one in which the anxieties we have to face, and the efforts we're called upon to make, feel required in the service of a task that makes sense to us.

Our career is the most poignant of topics because it is how we chart the interaction of who we are and what the world is; we're looking for the place where the best in us meets with the receptivity of the community. Where can our particular characteristics and aptitudes mesh satisfyingly and productively with the needs of others? Where can the labour of our lives best be deployed?

Instructions on how to fill in this book

Throughout these pages you will find sections highlighted in maroon.

Take time to fill in as many exercises as feels comfortable.

Do not worry if you fall behind.

The Pledge

Thinking about one's career can be terrifying: there is so much potential for regret, for present dismay and for anxiety about the future; there are so many reasons for panic and despair. The spirit of this book is not to deny the terror, but to hold onto the wider fact that we can also start to ask less frightened, more constructive questions. This spirit is encapsulated in the following affirmations, and we'd love you to embrace them as we do.

I accept that understanding what, for me, might be a good career direction is a large, complex, long-term question, deserving and requiring the better moments of my thought. I won't reserve it for expletives and grumbling.

Understanding my potential around work isn't about naming a specific kind of job I should be aiming at.

I accept that no job is perfect and that interesting work is also often difficult work.

I'm looking for work that is right for me, rather than a job that fits what other people might imagine or expect I should be doing.

I won't merely regret the choices I've made up to now and the experiences I've had. I will try to learn from (rather than resent) what went wrong; I will be curious about myself, rather than condemnatory.

I accept that career insight can come from unexpected places and that my childhood self may have something interesting to add to the conversation.

At some level I can bear to accept that all careers – even the apparently most successful – are failures; that the imaginative and emotional longings of human beings always outstrip the practical opportunities. It is very strange to be alive.

A career is a lifelong concern. It doesn't go away, and nor should it, because at every stage of existence it's properly noble – and inescapably difficult – to ask: what should I be doing with who I now am?

I believe in evolution rather than revolution: better isn't going to be accomplished in five dramatic minutes. The narrative of an existence is long; profound chances don't necessarily show up immediately on the surface.

The dominant image of work in our society today is a local snapshot of the vast reality of what it has been in the past and might be in the future. I know that doesn't mean I can change the world in which I happen to live, but this idea gives me perspective. I don't accept that our world is always right about what it celebrates and rewards. I will try to judge for myself.

Signed:

1.
Sympathy for Oneself

We should start with a little compassion for the moment we find ourselves in. For most of the history of humanity, the idea that we might seek to be happy at work – rather than just attempting to survive – would have sounded bizarre in the extreme.

Yet for the past 200 or so years, we have fallen for a highly demanding ideology that has promoted the concept that we might enjoy our jobs – and should consider ourselves freakish if we haven't been able to find an occupation that deeply fulfils us.

It sounds charitable, but it also places an enormous burden of expectation on us – and therefore renders us liable to disappointment and feelings of persecution and failure. We have become the prisoners of our very high expectations.

We might begin by reflecting on how nice it might, in a way, have been to have no option other than to suffer at work.

If you weren't able to pick a job on the basis that it would ever bring you pleasure, if you simply needed to do it for money and for status, what job would you choose?

....

....

What might you (nevertheless) find satisfying or somehow relaxing about your less-than-totally enjoyable job?

....

....

....

....

2.
Taking the Sunday Blues Seriously

Often, if we're having trouble with our careers, we get the Sunday blues.

They descend, normally, between around 5 p.m. and 7.30 p.m. and they can be at their height at 6 p.m., especially when the weather is grey and rainy.

The Sunday evening feeling is ordinarily associated with the idea of going back to work after a pleasant break. But this doesn't quite cover the complexity of what is going on: it isn't just that we have work to do that is dragging down our mood, but that we are going back to what might be the wrong sort of work, even while we are in dire ignorance of what the right sort of work might actually be.

We all have inside us what we might term a 'true working self': a set of inclinations and capacities that long to exert themselves on the raw material of reality. We want to turn the vital bits of who we are into jobs and ensure that we can see ourselves reflected in the services and products we are involved in turning out. This is what we understand by the right job, and the need for one is as fundamental and as strong in us as the need to love. We can be as broken by a failure to find our professional destiny as to identify an intimate companion. Feeling that we are in the wrong job, and that our true vocation lies undiscovered, is not a minor species of discomfort: it will be the central existential crisis of our lives.

We normally manage to keep the insistent calls of the true working self at bay during the week. We are too busy and too driven by an immediate need for money. But it reliably comes to trouble us on Sunday evenings. Like a ghost suspended between two worlds, it has not been allowed to live or to die, and so bangs at the door of consciousness, requiring a resolution. We are sad or panicked because a part of us recognises that time is running out and that we are not presently doing what we should with what remains of our lives. The anguish of Sunday evening is our conscience trying to stir us inarticulately into making more of ourselves.

In this sense, Sunday evenings have a history. Until recently, the last 200 years or so, there was – for most of us – no question of our true working selves ever finding expression in our labours. We worked to survive and would be grateful for a minimal income. But such reduced expectations no longer hold. We know – because there are enough visible examples of people who have done so – that we could harness our talents to the engines of commerce. We know that we don't have to be unhappy in this area, which adds a feeling of particular shame if we still are.

We should not be so hard on ourselves. We don't yet have all the mechanisms in place to unite ourselves with our purpose. It is in the nature of our working selves to be both clear in their dissatisfactions and yet maddeningly oblique about their real direction. We can be both utterly sure that we are not doing what we should, while also being wholly at sea about our genuine purpose.

The answer is patience, structure and steadfast intent. We need some of the discipline of the detective, or an archaeologist reassembling the pieces of a smashed jar. We should not dismiss our angst blithely as 'the Sunday blues', to be assuaged with a drink and a film. We should see it as belonging to a confused yet utterly central search for a real self that has been buried under a need to please others and to take care of short-term needs for status and money.

In other words, we should not keep our Sunday blues simply for Sunday evenings. We should place these feelings at the centre of our lives and let them be the catalysts for a sustained exploration that continues throughout the week, over months and probably years, and that generates conversations with ourselves, with friends, mentors and professionals. Something very serious is going on when sadness and anxiety descend for a few hours on Sunday evenings. We're not just a bit bothered to have to end two days of leisure; we're being driven usefully to distraction by a reminder to try to discover who we really are – and to do justice to our true talents – before it is too late.

Plan to convert your Sunday blues into something more fruitful

1. Recognise the origins of the anxiety: Sunday evenings aren't gloomy for no reason. Define as clearly as possible the nature of your career difficulties.

....

....

....

....

2. Give more time to the anxiety: pledge to stop leaving career anxiety for Sunday evenings only. Make more of your anxiety, not less. What other moments in the week could you also devote to your career thoughts?

Mon	Tue	Wed
Thu	Fri	Sat

3. Invite others into the anxiety: who going forward could you talk to about your career anxieties, rather than just turning them over in your own mind?

....

....

....

4. Look forward to a day when Sunday evenings might not be so painful. How would you like to feel during those times?

....

....

....

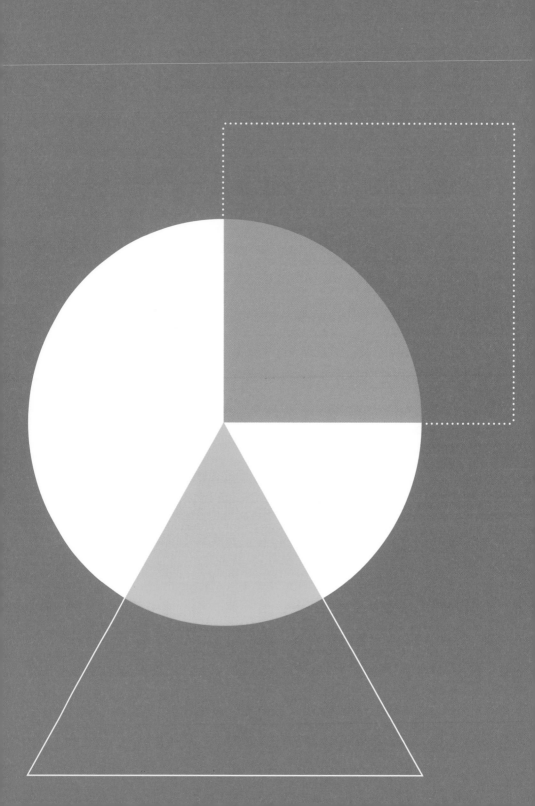

3.
The Clues of Childhood

Our search is for work that we can love – not work that has a lot of status attached to it or that pays well – and so we need to get to know a lot about what we love before we move too quickly towards formulating a career plan.

Childhood is the storehouse of incidental career insights because it was a time when we were able to engage with activities for their own worth, rather than because of social or financial pressures. Childhood reveals what we instinctively like, rather than what we've come to feel we should like. It's when no one cared what we were doing that we probably stumbled upon the real clues as to what we *should* now be doing.

We can get a powerful glimpse of how much of ourselves is already there in childhood when we consider the childhoods of people who have gone on in later life to establish very successful careers that seem exceptionally well suited to them as individuals.

The school report for a 7-year-old interested in nature might have read: 'David is quietly confident, greatly interested in animals and rocks and prone to forming strong opinions. He enjoys learning and expressing his views. He's adventurous but likes to have a goal. He's surprisingly canny, with a strong sense of initiative, and he is very earnest.'

Eventually, David Attenborough went on to have a hugely influential career as a nature broadcaster. His career developed out of the building blocks of potential that were already present in sketchy form in his childhood character.

David Attenborough filming *Life in The Undergrowth*, 2005

Or, imagine the report of 11-year-old Barbara: 'She likes going on long car rides through the countryside with her father, looking at the hills and the clouds. She enjoys drawing and is good at playing the piano (she has a very sensitive touch on the keys). She loves watching the waves on holiday at the seaside and has a collection of rocks and shells on a shelf by her desk. She enjoys rubbing them together or stroking them against her cheek. She's very diligent.'

Barbara Hepworth went on to become one of the leading British artists of the 20th century. As a child she couldn't make great works of art, but in adult life she was activating and putting to work her childhood passions and interests. She turned her daydreams about waves and clouds into objects that other people could admire.

We tend to revere people like Hepworth and Attenborough on the basis of their extraordinary talent – but maybe it's not just that. What really matters is that they refused to be separated from their passions and interests on the perilous journey from childhood to adulthood.

Barbara Hepworth working in her studio, 1963

Let's enter into a slightly meditative state. When, during our long childhood years, did we feel particular tremors of excitement? We should let our minds relax and offer up the smallest, most incidental details.

- Perhaps it was lovely lying on the bedroom floor in our old house (we must have been 8 years old), cutting out pieces of paper from a coloured pad and arranging alternating strips.
- Perhaps we loved getting breakfast ready for everyone (we especially enjoyed putting some fruit on top of the porridge).
- Perhaps we loved creating flying machines that we would launch from the top of the house.
- Perhaps we enjoyed making biscuits and selling them outside the front door.

The childhood play exercise

1. Remember five activities or games you enjoyed as a child. (e.g. playing with Lego.)

2. Try to identify the underlying enjoyment beneath each of the five activities. Complete the sentence: 'I enjoyed this because ...' (e.g. I enjoyed this because I loved creating streets and moving people around in them.)

1.

I enjoyed this because ...

2.

I enjoyed this because ...

3.

I enjoyed this because ...

4.

I enjoyed this because ...

5.

I enjoyed this because ...

3. Extrapolate your answers into adult character traits. Complete the sentence: 'I'm someone who likes …' (e.g. I'm someone who likes building an ordered system.)

I'm someone who likes …

I'm someone who likes …

I'm someone who likes …

I'm someone who likes …

I'm someone who likes …

What you've written down is likely to be very rich in clues. Your answers contain – in embryo – one key part of a self-portrait of your interests and passions.

4.
The Twelve Pleasure Points of Work

We know that work can in theory be enjoyable, but we're seldom encouraged to isolate and analyse what we can term the distinctive *pleasure points* offered by different jobs. We operate with a general sense that it might be nice to work as, say, a pilot, or to run a hotel, be a vet or make television shows, yet we are shy to drill into the specifics of where the pleasurable seams within such occupations might lie. We recognise that not even the best jobs can be enjoyable all the time, boredom and frustration will mar many a day, but in so far as any job can engage us sufficiently, it will tend to be because of a handful of specific sorts of moments of heightened gratification and delight that exist within it – and which are in synch with central aspects of our personalities.

Yet it is uncommon for us to split open jobs in search of these pleasure points or indeed to know our own sensitivities to different examples. We tend to understand quite a lot about what people do, but not so much about what there is to enjoy about given occupations – and because of this silence, we can find it hard to gauge where our working tastes might best be met.

We need to start to understand ourselves in terms of the pleasure points to which we are most receptive – and then sift through the labour market according to where given pleasures are likely to lie. However specific a job might be, the underlying pleasure points it yields tend to be capable of being filed under some general categories. When we stop focusing on the externals of salary or technical prerequisites, we can start to talk of any job as a distinctive constellation of pleasure points.

The task feels tricky because we don't yet have to hand a vocabulary of pleasure – but if we were to start the task of drawing one up, we would arrive at a list of twelve factors that tend to explain what it is people are implicitly alluding to when they say, in a surface way, that they 'love' their job.

No job will have all twelve pleasure points together, or in equal measure, so a central aspect of knowing one's working identity is to determine what one's own hierarchy of satisfaction might look like. As we read through a list of pleasure points, we'll realise that certain of these options will speak much more loudly to us than others. We can then start to rank them in order of preference. Our tastes might surprise us. Unexpected themes may emerge, and priorities change along with them. By taking a pulse of our responses to different pleasure points, we'll be granted material with which to start to draw up our own private template of what we need to look for in a job we may one day come to love.

1. The pleasure of making money

- You loved the time when you were 9 and made biscuits for a stall and sold them to people and turned a profit; it wasn't really the money, it was the excitement of seeing that people really liked what you'd done and were happy to prove it by giving up something unambiguously valuable. Next time you added different coloured icing – it was fascinating to see which colours people went for and which didn't appeal. You learned and it made you confident.

- You get a thrill out of guessing correctly what other people require; though it's not just guesswork, of course, it's because you're always on the lookout for little revealing signals that people don't even know they are sending. You love profit because it is, in many ways, an achievement of psychology: the reward for correctly guessing the needs of others ahead of the competition.

- You wander through the world aware of how much could be altered: if you walk along a street you might think: *That early 20th-century eyesore could be flattened, and a block of beautiful brick buildings put up in its place.* You notice a pile of cardboard boxes waiting to be recycled and think, *Isn't there some other use for these?* You grasp that every inefficiency is a business waiting to be born.

- The special appeal of money for you is the endorsement it brings of your insights and skills; you love how the fact that this year's profits are higher than the one before is a confirmation that you were clearly right in a myriad of little decisions you took over many months. It is the clearest proof of the soundness of judgement.

- Not everyone sees this, but for you, making money is an intellectual pleasure. You enjoy understanding your clients' needs at times better than they do themselves; you like coming up with a solution to a problem before other people have even quite realised there is a problem to be solved.

- You like that making money is connected to a set of down-to-earth virtues: understanding, hard work, efficiency, discipline and canniness.

- You know it is nice to have a bit of money (it's pleasant using an express lane at the airport and having the means to buy a work of art at a friend's exhibition) but you are clear in your own mind that this isn't a pleasure of working – it's a pleasure that comes as a consequence of work. What you enjoy about your job is the process of generating a profit by applying your insights to the problems of the world.

2. The pleasure of beauty

- You like it when a table is nicely laid: the way an elegant water glass harmonises with a well-designed knife and fork and a very plain earthenware plate. If a candlestick is placed off centre, you feel compelled to move it to the right position.

- As a child, you had a watch that you loved because the strap was a compelling colour: dark green with small red squares in a line down the middle; you loved wrapping birthday presents for your parents very carefully and got bothered when you couldn't fold the ends neatly; you always wanted to use the minimum pieces of sticky tape (three small strips), not out of a worry it might run out but because you loved (though you'd not have been able to articulate this at the time) the feeling that the least was also the best; you envied a friend's bike because the wheels were a slightly unusual size and this seemed to suit their personality; you loved watching boys who were good at playing football – you were struck by their different styles: one made lots of very rapid, small, nervy movements keeping the ball close to his feet, another took long loping strides and had a way of leaning back when taking a big kick.

- At school you loved carefully underlining the title of an essay; one year you experimented with wavy lines, at another point you used a ruler and obsessed about the thickness of the line. Sometimes you spent so long getting the title right you didn't have much time left for actually doing the writing.

- You notice when two buildings are misaligned, it spoils the street and you wish someone had taken more care and noticed how jarring the conjunction is; you wish you could go back in time and put it right.

- You like the look in winter of a brown ploughed field that leads to a line of grey, leafless trees on the horizon.

- You notice and appreciate a nice font on the pages of a book about German history.

- You might enjoy a film because it has lovely interior shots (you are paying attention to the shape of a room, the placing of furniture, the curve of a door handle) and for this you will forgive improbable convolutions of the plot or uninspired dialogue.

- You notice how much more excited you have been than any of your partners when the hotel room is just right.

3. The pleasure of creativity

- You were 7; all the Lego pieces were on the floor. Strangely, this was one of the best moments, as all the possibilities of the lovely things you might make were there somewhere. You were entranced by the potential. You loved cutting up cardboard boxes (the serrated edge of a bread knife was ideal for the task), and there was a memorable time when a washing machine arrived in one so big you wanted to live in it; you made a window flap and stocked the box with blankets, pillows and a bar of milk chocolate.

- You sometimes wish your favourite songs were a bit different – maybe they should repeat a particularly nice bit, or make their voices go down instead of up at the end; you want to fiddle with it (even though it is lovely already).

- As a child, at night before you went to sleep you used to imagine different things happening to your favourite characters in a story – how would it have been if they hadn't missed the train and maybe had a whole set of other, even more interesting adventures?

- In your sexual fantasies, you're always telling yourself stories about the broader lives of the protagonists, how they dress at work, what the layout of their apartment is, how they felt when they ordered a whip online; sometimes you realise you've even stopped thinking about sex.

- You love to be asked to imagine and assess the future: should we go into the American market? Is it worth making greetings cards? Should we get involved with the Turkish company? These sort of thought experiments come easily to you. Sometimes, you like to imagine what the ideal education system or the perfect city might be like.

- You enjoy considering which images will work best with a presentation, you are always trying to come up with better ways of conveying information; one time you hit upon a photo of a hippo up to its ears in a river to get your colleagues to see the urgency of an issue.

- People think you like novelty for its own sake, they couldn't be more wrong; you like better solutions, you just know that they often lie in unexpected places and you love hunting them down.

4. The pleasure of understanding

- You used to bother your parents with (in retrospect) slightly nonsensical questions: why are birds called 'birds', not something completely different like 'lotheropsicals'? What would baby chimpanzees look like if they were shaved? Do they have time on other planets? You wanted there to be good reasons for things.

- You were a bit shocked when you realised your father couldn't really explain why plugging in the hairdryer made it work. How could something coming out of the wall force the little fan to turn around?

- One time when you were 11, a friend said she was jealous of her sister. You were entranced by the way this idea could make sense of why someone got angry a lot with someone else.

- You love to lay down your thoughts on paper. Your mind becomes clearer to you and your anxiety levels decrease. Some people drink or go jogging to relax. You like to reflect.

- At school you hated it when the maths teacher said she couldn't tell you at the moment why this way of tackling a problem actually worked, all you needed to know was that it did; you felt cheated.

- You like it when a news report goes behind the scenes and explains why a particular compromise was reached, or why a party made a particular U-turn on its housing policy; it stops being a mystery (you dislike people who like mysteries) and starts to makes sense.

- You often feel people leave things unresolved; they don't explain properly, they don't seem curious about the multiple possible explanations about why people act as they do.

- You like it when a mass of seemingly conflicting facts can be given a coherent explanation. There's usually an underlying, much simpler and clearer, pattern waiting to be discovered.

5. The pleasure of self-expression

- As a child you liked it when adults asked your opinion (though sometimes you got frustrated because you didn't know what your opinion was on something, but you really wanted to have one).

- When you were in a play at school you loved the way you could expand – via a character – on a bit of yourself.

- You get frustrated when people don't listen, you want to make them pay attention.

- Some people think you are narcissistic, but they aren't actually right. It's that you love sharing things you like with others – it's not self-regard, it's a kind of generosity.

- There was one job you did where a senior manager took you aside after a meeting and told you that you should pipe down a bit, because what you thought wasn't always especially relevant to the agenda; later you could see their point but it really upset you.

- Sometimes on feedback forms you run out of space.

- You love it when people ask you good questions about yourself.

- The idea of writing an autobiography has crossed your mind.

- You'd adore to be interviewed, but find watching interviews often excruciating, you want to shout out: get to the juice, say the real stuff!

- When you do something, you want it to be obvious to others that you have done it.

- The idea that you could put your personality into making something – a chair, a garden, a government policy – strikes you as strangely alluring.

- You love it when you feel you have 'touched someone's soul'.

6. The pleasure of technology

- When you were little your aunt gave you a set of screwdrivers arranged according to size from micro to jumbo; you hardly ever used them but you loved the sense that each one was designed to tackle a slightly different problem, which sadly rarely came your way – though there was one lovely moment when there was a problem with a hinge in a kitchen cabinet door and your mother said, 'Where's that little set of screwdrivers of yours?' and you found one that fitted exactly (it was a 3mm Phillips head).

- When you were around 6 you stopped taking cars for granted and instead started to think of them as machines. It was amazing that there were these metal boxes decked out with special dials and little screens and windows that – unlike at home – would open at the touch of a button – or not if your mother had disabled the back ones. You were intrigued by exhaust pipes and radiator grills, which hinted at the strange needs of the machine.

- You love the idea that we are still at the beginning of the project of meeting our needs through technology. You like to imagine where we might be by 2180.

- You don't necessarily think of technology just as machines and information processing; the pencil appeals to you as a model of technology: simple, intuitive, robust, perfect for its function (you secretly love pencil sharpeners and sometimes might sharpen a pencil just for the pleasure of using this perfect little mechanism and seeing a crisp little curl of wood roll off the blade); in your eyes, socks are wearable foot technology.

- You hate it when people associate the future with jetpacks. It will be far more interesting than that.

- You love asking 'What's the essence of this problem and how could it be solved more cheaply and easily?'

7. The pleasure of helping other people

- As a child you loved being allowed to join in. Your sister hated being asked to unload the dishwasher, but you rather liked it because you felt you were contributing. You liked the feeling that your parents could be getting on with cooking the rice or phoning the plumber because you'd freed them up.

- In make-believe games you liked rescue scenarios; someone was going to be eaten by piranhas and you'd pull them back onto the raft (which was actually a sofa) just in time.

- You like it when friends tell you what is bothering them. You don't always know what to do, but you like trying to say comforting things (and sometimes you feel very upset when they reject your well-intended comments).

- You feel that work is meaningful because it makes a difference to other people; in some way it brings them pleasure or solves a problem they have, and you really like hearing about this. You like the idea of seeing the consequences of what you do in the lives of others.

- Your father used to get frantic when he thought he'd lost the car keys; you liked being the one who could calm him down and say 'Think, what did you do when you came home yesterday evening?' Once he found them in the bathroom.

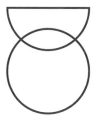

8. The pleasure of leading

- You didn't just *want* to be in charge, you actually *liked* being in charge (it was a difference that struck you early). Lots of people at school wanted to be picked as the team captain but they didn't really like the responsibility, they just wanted the status. What you wanted was the job, the role, the chance to put your ideas into practice.

- You like it when others turn to you for advice. You don't just say whatever comes into your head. You want to solve their problems. You want them to be able to trust your judgment.

- You like it when leadership is earned, not just conferred.

- You enjoy hearing about leaders who haven't succeeded by ordinary standards; when you were about 14 you read a story about a general who surrendered to save the lives of the troops – they didn't win, but he was a real leader, you thought.

- When other people get in a panic you find yourself getting more focused; you like that about yourself.

- When people say they want to avoid responsibility if possible, your first instinct is to dislike them.

- When you were little you were excited by the idea of fame. It doesn't appeal much now, it just seems like an unfortunate side effect of being good at something.

9. The pleasure of teaching

- If someone makes a mistake you want to put them right.

- You had a lovely teacher when you were 7, she knew how carefully you were listening and when you were trying (even if you got something wrong).

- You love the feeling of equipping somebody else with your knowledge, and how you can turn their panic and frustration into mastery and confidence.

- You know you have to be careful where you deliver your 'lessons'; people don't like to feel patronised, but you like nothing more than filling in the gaps in the knowledge of others.

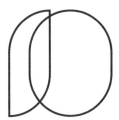

10. The pleasure of independence

- The first time you drove on your own, you never wanted to stop.

- You like getting up very early before anyone else is around; you can follow your own projects in peace and quiet.

- For you, growing up has been all about getting away from people who can control you.

- You like being alone; boredom rarely troubles you.

- You recoil from guided tours and tour groups.

- You were extremely excited when you read a story about a man who had quit his work in a bank and started a company importing avocadoes from West Africa.

- You really like coming to your own opinion about the merits of a book or a work of art and it doesn't much bother you if other people might regard you as a bit of an eccentric.

- You've been accused at times of not being a team player and to be honest there's a degree of truth in the criticism.

- An evening on your own is never a challenge. It gives you a chance to plot and to think. It annoys you how some people always just want to chatter.

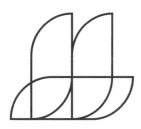

11. The pleasure of order

- When you were doing homework you really liked making your writing clear; if you had to rub out a mistake in pencil you were very careful that the rubbing out wasn't visible. You hated making mistakes in ink and experimented with pasting extra little bits of paper on top of a mistake so as to preserve an overall look of neatness.

- You were fascinated by the cutlery drawer; you loved the fact that each kind of thing had a special place. It bothered you a lot when your sister didn't care and sometimes dropped a spoon nonchalantly into the fork section.

- Even if you weren't very good at science you found the periodic table strangely alluring; you liked the idea of everything being sorted into their constituent elements and the chaos of the world being reduced down to a few elements only. This struck a chord, even if you found yourself looking out the window when the details were explained.

- You hate it when people say 'filing' in a sneering way.

- You like arranging sets of colouring pencils according to the colour spectrum … though there always seem to be some problems; does yellow shade into white or light green (via greenish yellow)?

- You get annoyed when people jump around telling a story ('Oh I forgot to mention …').

12. The pleasure of nature

- You can't bear how so many modern windows don't open.

- It was lovely, aged 8, to get down on your hands and knees and look closely at a hedgehog or a snail. You felt it could be your friend. You liked imagining its life, which seemed as interesting as any human's.

- You love camping, especially if the weather isn't perfect. It's more of an interesting challenge to put up a tent in a storm.

- You were on a long walk in the country with your family and it started to rain and everyone complained, but you loved it; you just drew up the hood of your cagoule and liked it when you could feel the raindrops landing on your nose.

- You had mixed feelings about watching David Attenborough documentaries: you found them very interesting, but you didn't just want to watch sitting on the sofa with a plate of fish fingers on your lap. You wanted to be there in the swamps of the Serengeti plains during the wet season or clambering over the rocks of the Galápagos Islands; you wouldn't care if you got mud up to your knees or scratched your fingers quite badly.

None of us ever identify equally with all these pleasures. Some stand out, and can perhaps move up our list of priorities. In the process of reading about them, we may start to discover our personal pleasure-point profile and know that these are the kinds of pleasures we should be looking for opportunities to develop in our working lives. In talking to others about their work, these are topics we should be probing. If we read about someone's career, we should be on the lookout for what has been pleasurable in their days and tracing where this might intersect with our own pleasure-needs. We're in search of the precious zone where our talents and pleasures meet the needs of the world – that is the place in which we should try so hard to locate our future careers.

Our personal pleasure-point profile

1. Read each pleasure point and see whether it touches on things that excite you or engage with your memories. In the categories that most appeal to you, think about details from your own life – things that you've enjoyed in the past or that have given you pleasure in work situations.

    It might take a little while for these to come to mind. Once the general idea of noting pleasures is in your mind you might – over the course of a few days – suddenly remember (when waiting to pay at the supermarket or when stopped at a traffic light) something you really liked when you were 10 that belongs somewhere on the following list. It can take ages to get to know the contents of our minds and working out what really gives us pleasure is a lifelong enquiry.

2. Having added our own thoughts to the list, some of these pleasures may stand out to you and others may leave you a bit cold. Write down the list of pleasures, with the most important to you at the top and the least important at the bottom.

In eventually settling on a particular job, you will have to make sacrifices. Each job will meet some pleasures more and others less – there may be creativity but less opportunity to lead; or plenty of time spent on understanding but few opportunities to help others. Ranking the pleasures will give you a statement of what you value most, and thus what you should seek in a job, if necessary, at the expense of other satisfactions.

3. Getting to know our pleasures is a key ingredient in working out what kind of job would fulfil us. But the pleasures on their own don't usually point to a specific line of work. What they do give us is a very good way of examining the suitability of any particular job that one might consider.

Select any job that's crossed your mind at any point as something you might be interested in doing (even if you never took it very seriously). Think about whether this job would offer much scope for the pleasures at the top of your list – the ones that matter most to you.

Even if you come to think that this job doesn't stack up at all well against your pleasure points, this is a valuable gain of knowledge. You'll have a much clearer sense of why this wouldn't be the right job for you.

Repeat the exercise for all the different jobs you've ever vaguely considered. Flick through the job section at the back of the paper. The goal is to get practiced at assessing possible jobs with respect to pleasure points.

5.
Jobs That Leave Me Cold

It might sound odd to bring this up, but not all jobs will interest you – even jobs that are ostensibly quite prestigious and well paid. The more you realise what you don't want to do, the more you will be nudged into realising what does appeal.

The process we're using is comparable to the way Michelangelo thought about his work as a sculptor. In his view, a statue is already latently inside every block of marble and has to be chipped away by the sculptor.

Michelangelo, *The Prisoners*, 1523

Our true working self is like an insight that has to be released. But in our case, the liberation of this self occurs not by using a mallet and chisel but by firing questions at our minds.

Write down ten jobs that strangers or acquaintances are pursuing that you yourself have no interest in.

Try to identify why these jobs leave you cold. Write down the things that you dislike about them in the second column.

Jobs that others are pursuing	Reasons why they leave me cold

6.
Lives That Make Me Envious

In our search for clues to our real passions and interests, we're going to turn to our feelings of envy.

A word of caution as we introduce the topic: in our society, envy has been taboo for at least two thousand years. Here is the representation of envy, or in Latin, *invidia*, by the great painter Giotto on the walls of the Arena Chapel in Padua, Italy, painted in 1306. *Invidia* was one of the Catholic Church's seven 'deadly sins' – and experiencing it was deemed a sure sign we were headed to hell.

No wonder many of us are still quite wary of registering the emotion.

Some of us may feel that we never feel envy, but such a thing isn't psychologically possible. Envy is normal, natural and even healthy. The trick isn't not to feel it, but to learn to use it well.

For our purposes, envy matters so much because it provides such rich insights into our passions and interests. Every time we envy someone, we are encountering a clue as to who we deep down really want to be – and in part probably could be.

We don't envy everyone. We envy those who we feel have what we deserve, are interested in – and could perhaps attain one day. Every person we envy contains clues as to who – in the Nietzschean sense – we 'really are' and should try to become.

Giotto, *Envy*, from
The Seven Vices, 1306

Unfortunately, we are extremely bad students of envy. The real problem isn't that we feel envy, but that we envy in such an unexamined way.

Why we are bad students of envy:

1. We feel deeply embarrassed by our envy, and so tend to hide the emotion from ourselves.

2. We don't think there is anything to be learnt from our envy, so we just hope the mood will pass, like a particularly bad kind of headache with no content for us to mine.

3. We get fixated on envying whole people. We say, without imagination, that we want to be just like them, or to have their life. But that's generally far too broad-brush. We need to find out a few focused things that are really powering our envy.

We want to teach you the art of decoding your envy. We start to envy certain individuals in their entirety, when in fact, if we took a moment to analyse their lives calmly, we would realise that it is only a small part of what they have done that really resonates with, and should guide, our own next steps.

It might not be the whole of the restaurant entrepreneur's life we want, but really just their skill at building up institutions.

We might not truly want to be a potter (when we think more closely about it), and yet we might need a little more of the playfulness on display in the work of one example we read about in a Sunday supplement.

We might not actually want to be a photographer and take photographs of life in deprived areas: the bit we really like is that this person is making a difference by showing the rich world how the poor world lives – a task that could be carried out in lots of different ways (some easier than trying to become a Magnum photographer).

Decoding your envy

1. List around four names in the column below titled 'People I envy'. Two might be people you've heard about in the media and public life, and two might be people you directly know, either well or just casually and distantly. Don't worry about the vagueness or peculiarity of the list. You might envy your sister, someone you met for two minutes in a nail bar or your boss.

2. In the second column, write down the achievements that they're most obviously known for.

3. The third column is trickier: 'The positive bits I don't really want'. It's an odd but true thought: even when we envy certain people, it isn't the whole of them we actually envy. We don't mean that there are inevitably going to be some downsides to their lives. We mean that among the upsides, not all elements are going to appeal to us. So, don't focus on the inconvenience of

1. People I envy	2. Their achievements
Steve Jobs	Creating the iPhone
Yvonne	A job in private equity

their job. Don't say 'the paparazzi' or 'the long hours'. Keep thinking of what is positive about their career or achievement but isn't actually for you.

This can be surprising. It might be that when it comes to a really rich person, the thing you don't especially want is their wealth. Or with a creative person, maybe it's not actually the art you want. It could be something else: the capacity to manage your own time or the ability to use a foreign language.

4. Finally, complete the column titled 'The positive bits I want'. This is the significant bit. The task is to extrapolate from the very specific life you've pinpointed a few things that really interest you; a few moves that these people are making that lie at the root of your feelings of excited discomfort and painful longing.

We've included a couple of examples in the table. Now try filling in your own.

3. The positive bits I don't really want	4. The positive bits I want
The management side	Marrying tech and beauty
A fancy office	Financial competence

7.
Clarification Exercise

We're going to try another exercise now. We can compare this exercise to another sequence of short little taps of a chisel against a block of marble; it will further help us to define the shape of our true interests and passions; it should help us to get a bit closer to becoming who we are.

The exercise on the next page involves studying a long list of binary oppositions of qualities or traits that your ideal job, product or service would involve. (You do not have to know what this job or product actually is – the idea here is to clarify what your interests are, not yet to decide on what your vocation should be.)

We can make an analogy here with a metal detector, scouring over the surface to try to determine the presence of precious materials below ground. If the exercise were a career metal detector, listening out for the precious metal of your ideal self, over what words and terms might it let out a particularly strong beep?

Take a look at the following table. It's made up of binary oppositions on every line. As you scan down, circle whichever of the two entries feels most relevant. If both feel relevant, circle them both, if neither do, leave them blank. Try to answer quickly. Do not pause to look for definitions of these words; answer intuitively, based on what the word means to you personally.

The ideal product or service for me to be involved in might be ...

Helping the mind	Helping the body
Must bring social recognition	Obscurity is OK
Long-term	Immediate
Costs a lot	Cheap
Helping the rich world	Helping the developing world
A problem of survival	A problem of complex modern life
Mass market	Niche
Created by a team	Created by me
Live	Recorded
Bringing excitement	Bringing reassurance
Entertaining	Useful
Scalable	One-off
Coloured by fashion	Enduring
Quick turnover	Long product cycle
Anonymous	Personally flavoured
For profit	For charity
Hands-on	At a distance
Big institution	Workshop
Entrepreneurial	Big system

Peer-evaluated	Market-evaluated
Business-to-consumer	Business-to-business
Big	Small
Words	Images
Hard-wearing	Fragile
Analogue	Digital
Innovative	Classical
Leader	Deputy
Public sector	Private sector
Intuitive	Procedural
OK if it takes a few decades	Short-term
Regulated	Unregulated
Market mature	Market open
Fluctuation	Stability
Leads to something else	An end in itself
Behind the scenes	Upfront
Sensory	Intellectual
Risky	Safe
Glamorous	Sober

Now take a moment to look back over the list and double circle six traits that are especially appealing to you.

8.
Visualisation Exercise

Sometimes, our senses know better than our rational minds what job might be suited for us.

Try to imagine a job of the future in terms of the visual appearance you'd like it to have. Would it be in an office, or a different location? What should the carpets be like? What would it smell like?

We've included some images of different workplaces to get you going. Give each image a score out of 10 in terms of desirability, with 10 being the most desirable.

① ② ③ ④ ⑤ ⑥ ⑦ ⑧ ⑨ ⑩

① ② ③ ④ ⑤ ⑥ ⑦ ⑧ ⑨ ⑩

① ② ③ ④ ⑤ ⑥ ⑦ ⑧ ⑨ ⑩

(1) (2) (3) (4) (5) (6) (7) (8) (9) (10)

Looking back at the images you rated highest in terms of desirability, what do these workplaces have in common?

_____

_____

_____

_____

Are there common themes in the images you rated the lowest? What makes these workplaces undesirable?

_____

_____

_____

_____

9.
An Advertisement for Myself

In 1959, the famously self-concerned but also inspiringly self-confident American writer Norman Mailer published a book titled *Advertisements for Myself*.

In it, Mailer explained who he was, what he wanted from life, how he saw his creative talent and what he hoped the world could understand about him. It was a hugely valuable exercise with relevance far beyond his particular case and with special application to the business of applying for jobs.

We should all, in a sense, write an 'advertisement' for ourselves. The idea sounds cheeky because of an unwarranted modesty on most of our parts. We don't believe we should be advertising ourselves at all: we simply wait for others to advertise their openings. But this is dangerously passive. The better we know what we could offer the world, the more the world might be ready to provide it. Not having a plan puts us recklessly at the mercy of the plans of others.

An advertisement for myself

My name is …

I'm not (though it would be convenient and I'd be capable of it) going to seek to become a …

because …

(You can fill in one of the jobs you chose for the exercise in chapter 5, on page 41.)

Deep down in my sincere self, I'm someone who likes:

1.

2.

3.

4.

5.

(You can use the five things you wrote for the childhood play exercise in Chapter 3, on page 19.)

I remember, as a child, much enjoying:

....

....

....

(You can use one of the activities you included in the childhood play exercise in Chapter 3, on page 18.)

Now what I want is an occupation which:

....

....

....

....

(You can use your answers from the far-right hand column, 'The positive bits I want', of the exercise in Chapter 6, on page 45.)

The pleasures that my job needs to deliver are:

1.

....

2.

....

3.

....

4.

....

(You might want to refer to the pleasures you ranked highest in the pleasure point profile exercise in Chapter 4, on page 38.)

Continued overleaf ↲

Key aspects of my ideal job are that it would be:

1.

2.

3.

4.

5.

6.

(You might want to refer to the six traits that you double ringed in the clarification exercise in Chapter 7, on page 48.)

Congratulations, you have now completed an advertisement for yourself. This is a very valuable document to keep with you and to look over in the days and weeks ahead.

Further exercise with friends

1. Invite a few friends over who are going through comparable dilemmas in their jobs.

2. All stand up and read your advertisements out to the group.

3. Say what your current job is, why you are a bit unhappy (if you are), and the rough areas you are thinking about for the future.

4. Having heard from a brave person, what can we collectively imagine them doing next in their professional lives?

You might discuss some of the following questions:

What kind of jobs might they do?

Were they surprised by any of the suggestions and why?

How do they feel about it now? (Do they perhaps feel like there are more options than they thought?)

This exercise gives us a chance to crowdsource career ideas based on our advertisement.

Be imaginative: consider jobs that are outside of the 9–5 rat race; jobs that do not take place in a normal office; jobs that perhaps require uniforms (or not); jobs that do not fall under the remit of the traditional professions.

Normally we expect employers to interview us. But in order to make full use of our pleasures and interests, we need to be armed with our advertisement for ourselves – and interview the world – so as to honour our greatest responsibility of all: to our own native talents and concerns.

10.
Family Scripts

In our discussions so far, the emphasis has been squarely on one particular part of the dilemma of modern work: how to discover our deep-seated but very shy and often unknown passions. Our efforts will hopefully have helped us to zero in on a list of these – and even to arrive at an ideal advertisement for ourselves, along with some jobs we might plausibly want to aim for.

But we have – deliberately – been ignoring one very important aspect of the puzzle: why, even when we know our interests and passions, do we show a remarkable capacity for not moving forward with them? What is holding us back?

Some of the obstacles are extremely practical – but, while we deeply respect these, they are not principally what interest us at The School of Life. Our emphasis, as we've mentioned at the start, is squarely on the *psychological obstacles* that prevent us from attaining our potential. It's to a range of these that we turn now.

In the following table, fill in the left-hand column with the career move you'd ideally want to make – for example, 'go into architecture' or 'start a business'. Then, in the right-hand column, write down the greatest insults you might tell yourself about that move when you're in a self-critical, hyper-realistic mood – for example, 'it's only for dreamers', 'that's what chancers think', 'how pretentious' or 'that's not for you'.

What I might want to be or do:	My greatest suspicion, fear or insults around it:

What interests us is where the insults and suspicions have come from. Inner voices were once outer voices around us. They are the judgements of others, which we've forgotten to notice are not entirely our own. Very often, they may be the voices of people who continue to have an overwhelming influence on our values and choices: members of our families.

One of the most stubborn psychological obstacles to progressing in our interests and passions can be traced back to our families. For most of human history, the working destiny of every new generation was automatically determined by the preceding generation. One would become a farmer or soldier like one's father, or a seamstress or teacher like one's mother. Choices were cruelly restricted and penalties for deviating from the intended trajectory could be severe.

Then, in the early 20th century, under the sway of a Romantic ideology, societies gradually freed themselves from class and parental strictures. We're now supposed to be able to do whatever job we want. We firmly believe we have been left alone to decide just as we please. In a sense, we have been.

But this idea of having been left alone has had the curious effect of hiding from us just how much familial expectations continue to operate in the background and to matter, and therefore to restrict the course of our careers – except that they do so without us realising. Love can control us as much as force or the law ever did.

In the back of our minds there are always what we can term 'family work scripts'. These scripts restrict what sorts of jobs we feel able to devote ourselves to and encourage us towards a set of favoured options. Our backgrounds make certain forms of work more or less available.

At the most benign level, our family work scripts are the result of what our families *understand* of the working world. Every family has a range of occupations that it grasps – because someone has practised them and, in the process, humanised them and brought them within the imaginative range of other family members.

There are families where, as long as anyone can remember, there have been doctors around. From a young age, one has heard about the often comedic habits of patients, the rivalries on the ward, the eccentricities of senior doctors and the fun and agony of medical school. It hence comes to feel normal and possible that one might, when the time comes, decide to join the ranks of the medical establishment.

Think about the work scripts that may be present in your own family and fill in the next table.

In my family, we understand these jobs:	In my family, we don't understand these jobs:

In many families, there will be certain career options that the parents speak about with particular reverence: perhaps being a great writer or a senior judge, a headmaster or a civil servant. These frequently aren't the jobs that the parents are themselves engaged in; they are what they once wanted to do (but never did).

Many parents quietly hand their dreams onto their children to fulfil – usually without telling them that they have placed these burdens on their shoulders. We're equally liable to receive little messages that certain careers are beneath us, dangerous, phoney or not quite right for our sort of station in life.

We should beware of the paradigm that parents are conservative and children are creative and romantic; that the child wants to be a pop star and the parents want them to be a dentist. In a notable number of cases, the suspicion runs another way: the child would quite like a steady, safe job, but it's the parents who are pushing them towards a grander, more insecure and more artistic or socially minded destiny.

Let's think more deeply about your family's expectations by filling in a third table.

What my family would have liked me to be:	What were they very anxious about around careers? What made them nervous?

Glance back at the first table and see if you can write the name of a family member beside the insults you have jotted down.

We should be extremely gentle on ourselves for the extent to which we are hemmed in by our family scripts. It is entirely natural that this should be so, given how many years we spent being dependent on our families, how much they (probably) loved us and how receptive children always are to the messages around them. At the same time, we should build up an awareness of what belongs to them and what belongs to us. However much we owe our families, we do not owe them our whole lives. They may understand a lot about us, but not everything. We may in certain areas simply need to break with their paradigms and expectations. We may need to risk their love and approval for the sake of an even greater responsibility: our own career aspirations.

We should also realise how, in a bid to stay loyal to our families, we may have been self-sabotaging our careers, almost deliberately failing in order to succeed at the task of loyalty. We should recognise how unnerving satisfaction can feel in relation to our loved ones. The prospect of a satisfying career, when it eventually appears, can seem counter-intuitive and not a little frightening. We should start to get suspicious when we catch ourselves pulling off poor performances around people we need to impress, or not going for opportunities that would be perfectly well within our grasp. We may be trying to stay loyal to people who loved us but could not necessarily understand what we really needed.

There is another way in which the family script operates. Many of us carry within us a strong desire to do better than our families: this can guide our choices just as powerfully as our wish to fit in with our families. Traditionally, that has meant the wish to make more money than our parents, but in many countries that's not going too well nowadays. The term can also be applied to situations in which we seek to gain some nonmaterial advantage over the previous generation – perhaps our lives can be more creative, more loving or more leisure-filled than theirs.

How do you desire to do better than other members of your family?
Complete the following table.

My family didn't succeed at …	I would be doing better than my family if I …

We're pitching this in terms of rivalry, but we may also harbour a secret, tender and loving wish to 'heal' the previous generation: to correct some of the psychological compromises, blind spots or excesses of our parents through our work. There will most likely always be something missing from, or damaged about, the life experience of those who brought us up.

- Perhaps our father wasn't having enough fun. Perhaps he was scarred by financial instability when he was little and that's why he judged work primarily in terms of security.
- Perhaps our mother was a bit frantic in her search for adventure – in reaction to her own excessively stultifying upbringing.

So, a career choice is at some level often semiconsciously guided by a desire to heal aspects of our parents' psyches. One might be trying to demonstrate, for instance, that it is possible to care about stability *and* have a personally meaningful career, or that one can be a person with a soul *and* also be interested in worldly success. One may want to show that one can manage to do well in finance *and* at the same time be close to one's children. Or thoughtful *and* interested in science.

We are vitally spurred on by attempts to go beyond the limitations of our parents.

A discussion with oneself

How might we want to exceed our parents psychologically – at the level of maturity and happiness – through our work?

....

....

....

....

What would it mean to put right the errors of thinking and feeling of the previous generation?

....

....

....

....

How could we help our parents (even if they are dead or not especially interested in our assistance; the unconscious doesn't tend to factor in such details)?

....

....

....

....

....

11.
Supportive and Unsupportive People

We might presume that everyone around us wants us to thrive. But sometimes a change of career on our part may – for a variety of reasons – be problematic for a few people around us.

People are often silently held together by shared fears and vulnerabilities. Our acquaintances may well say that anything we do will be fine by them, but in reality certain decisions can undermine their own life choices. For example, if we are leaving academia to go into business, might that throw into doubt certain choices our fellow academics have made?

Let's put it another way: who energises you in your search for new work? And who drains you?

We're going to conclude with a sobering truth: changing jobs may involve changing friends.

Supportive and unsupportive people

In order to find our true career self, we may need to distance ourselves from a few people who do not wish to accept our new persona. We should ask ourselves two useful questions:

Who around me may not be supportive of my passions and interests?

Who around me is really supportive?

12.
Self-sabotage

It's natural to expect that we instinctively want to win and be successful. But there's something odd about human nature. What we feel confident about achieving is to a great extent determined by a prior sense of what we feel we deserve to have and to be in this world. The more confident we are about deserving a lot, the more confident we'll be in fighting for it.

We all operate with a background sense – normally unconscious – of what we deserve:

- how much money we might have
- how well-known we might be
- how successful we might be at work

Importantly, this sense of what we deserve doesn't come first and foremost from us: it is an internalisation of what other people thought we deserved, usually our parents, when we were little.

We have grown up with a sense of deserving certain things – and not deserving others. We might expect that no one would ever put a limit on anyone else's sense of deserving anything – especially their own child. But in fact, without in any way being cruel or nasty, our caregivers often put a limit on our hopes. We may have heard, in childhood, the idea that: 'People like us don't do or have X …'

What messages did your caregivers quietly send out about what you deserved?

....

....

....

....

....

Why did our caregivers limit our hopes?

- They may have had a caste-like view of society: some people get big things, but not people like us, they hinted.
- They were trying to protect one of your siblings, who might have been threatened or dethroned by your success.
- They might have felt painfully threatened if we had got more than they ever had: their fear was that we might no longer think well of them or want to see them.
- If we got more than they did, they were afraid it would remind them – uncomfortably – of the extent to which they didn't achieve very much.

For such understandable reasons, even very nice people can end up limiting what we feel we deserve and how confident we can be about getting it. Having a background set of limited expectations can spark what we call self-sabotage whenever we get close to success.

Self-sabotage is an attempt to bring our external reality back in line with what we feel we inwardly deserve. There are many examples of self-sabotage. The mechanism operates so cleverly, most of us don't even realise we're doing it:

- When someone we really like is keen back ... we act aggressive and sour on the next date.
- When we are in line for promotion ... we flirt with the boss's partner at the office party.
- When we acquire a great social life ... we pit one friend against another.
- When we get a big contract ... we procrastinate fatefully.

In all cases, what we're trying to do is to ensure that we don't get any more than we feel deep down that we deserve. We sabotage ourselves until the outer world doesn't give us more than the inner world says we deserve.

There are spectacular cases of this happening with celebrities – who appear to blow up flourishing careers seemingly for no reason. There can be many causes of this, but self-sabotage is likely to be one of them.

What is the solution to the impulse to self-sabotage?

Firstly: we should take an audit of what we feel we deserve that was created in childhood.

Secondly: we should – if necessary – liberate our sense of what we deserve from those childhood limitations.

We need to believe that we can *create*, rather than *inherit*, our sense of what we deserve. That was impossible when we were 5 or 15. It is now – at our age – very possible. We can be the authors of our own ideas of what we deserve.

We can try an exercise to help identify and loosen the hold of our inherited expectations.

Inherited expectation exercise

How has your background limited the expectations you are allowed to have?

....

....

....

....

....

Does it feel dangerous or peculiar to want certain things? What are you afraid of when you hope for more?

....

....

....

....

....

....

....

Are you aware of self-sabotaging?

....

....

....

....

....

....

Now complete the following sentence:

I feel I should, from now on, allow myself to believe I deserve ...

....

....

....

....

....

....

....

What we're realising is that we are not merely underconfident by chance. We are often underconfident to ensure that we never achieve more than we feel we deserve. But what we feel we deserve can, and in some cases *must,* be changed.

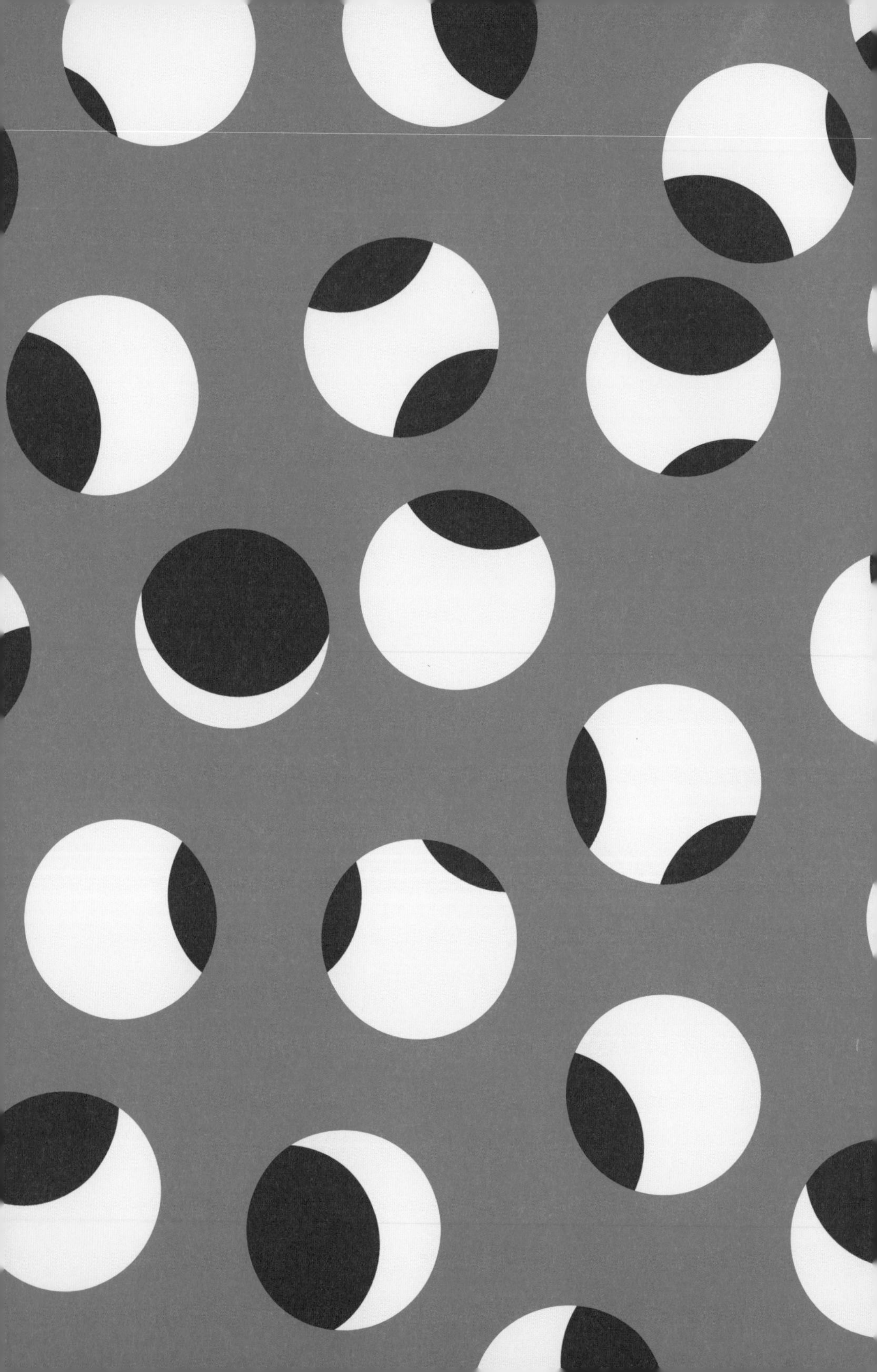

13.
Fixation and Unfixation

One key thing that can go wrong in our thinking about a career is that we get fixated on a particular kind of job which – for one reason or another – turns out not to be a promising or realistic option. It may be that the job is extremely difficult to secure, it may require long years of preparation or it might be in an industry that has become precarious and therefore denies us good long-term prospects.

Here we call it a fixation – rather than simply an interest – to signal that the focus on the job is proving problematic because we have an overwhelming sense that our future lies with this one occupation and this occupation alone – while nevertheless facing a major obstacle in turning our idea into a reality.

The solution to such fixations lies in coming to understand more closely what we are really interested in. The more accurately and precisely we fathom what we care about, the more we can find our interests in diverse places. It's a lack of understanding of what we're really after which gets us fixated on certain jobs.

The careful investigation of what we love in one field of work shows us – paradoxically, but very liberatingly – that we could in fact also love working in a slightly different field.

We may find that what we really love isn't this specific job, but a range of qualities we have first located there, normally because this job was the most conspicuous example of a repository of them – which is where the problem started because over-conspicuous jobs tend to attract too much attention, get over-subscribed and are then in a position to offer only very modest salaries.

Yet in reality, the qualities can't only exist there. They are necessarily generic and will be available under other, less obvious guises – once we know how to look.

Antifixation exercise

In the first column below, we've listed jobs that some people might desperately crave. Then as we move towards the right, we boil down what they really want and then see where else it might be found.

Let's begin the exercise by filling in the two missing gaps in column 4 below.

1. Where I want to work	2. What I'd enjoy	3. Pleasure involved	4. Where else the pleasure might be found
Goldman Sachs	Closing the deal	Negotiation	Bank, antique furniture store, small claims court, HR hiring team
UNICEF	Helping in disasters	Caring for others	Nursing assistant for the elderly, flight attendant, AA highway assistance, firefighter
Universal Studios	Designing film sets	Visual and spatial creativity	
The New York Times	Writing articles	Self-expression, analysis, understanding	

Now answer the same questions for yourself. Start by writing down a job that appeals to you.

Then, analyse what it is within this job that you'd especially enjoy. Stop thinking in terms of institution or sector; start thinking (as we've taught you) in terms of your pleasures.

Try to generalise outwards from the specific pleasure to the general category of pleasure. Move from saying 'designing film sets' to 'visual and spatial creativity.'

Finally, imagine other places where the qualities that attract you might lie.

1. Where I want to work

2. What I'd enjoy

3. Pleasure involved

4. Where else the pleasure might be found

14.
Evolution Not Revolution

When we're thinking of making a shift in career, we can easily get dismayed by the scale of the change we're contemplating. We imagine change in dramatic, volcanic terms. We feel we're looking at a revolution in our lives. Everything will have to be different – and that's often a very daunting and unwelcome prospect.

We should recognise that our picture of what change might look like and how it might take place can become a problematic, inhibiting factor. We may stick with what is familiar because the only kind of change we can imagine is revolution. We're guided by the natural (but mistaken) notion that if change is going to occur at all, it's going to have to look dramatic.

Imagine changing your life to become an architect and picture the most dramatic changes you'd need to make – changes like resigning tomorrow, going back for seven years of education and so on. Of course, when change is envisaged like this, it's no wonder that we may choose not to do anything at all. We're being too extreme – and therefore altering nothing.

At The School of Life, we firmly believe that a career change can best happen via a process of evolution.

- You don't have to quit your job right now.
- Your parents and partners don't need to know.
- Your friends don't need to know.
- Nothing needs to change.

Revolution	Evolution
Quit job	Learn architectural drawing from an online course
Sign up for a seven-year architecture degree	Sketch one new building every weekend
Move house, take the children out of school	Take an architect out for lunch and chat properly

Choose a career move or a job that sounds appealing to you and write it in the 'Revolution' column in the next table. In the 'Evolution' column, think of small steps you could take to move towards this goal. These steps should involve minimal financial outlay and few visible moves.

Revolution	Evolution

Minor moves can strengthen our courage by giving us a sense of a talent in an area where we as yet have very little experience. They break through the unhelpful but widely prevalent sense that we should either remain as we are or change everything. In reality, there is a far less glamorous, more neglected third option we must explore: the careful evolutionary step.

The great thing about the evolutionary approach is that we can try out many career roles for size simultaneously. We do not commit to any one path fully. Rather, we can undertake small, low-risk experiments for several different potential careers at the same time – ditching those we find unsatisfactory and gradually increasing the dedication and energy we apply to the most satisfying.

15.
We Are (Sort of) Free

There are – of course – so many obstacles to making a change. We know that. Let's think about what they might be.

Obstacles to change

Money	Length of training
Left it too late	Not the right background
Too busy	Not the right school
Children	No openings
Partner or spouse	Impossible odds
State of the economy	Not enough experience
Parents	No contacts

Try thinking of a few obstacles of your own:

All of these are hugely legitimate obstacles that it would be deeply foolish to ignore, belittle or gloss over.

Nevertheless, there's one obstacle that's larger than any of the others. It takes up a disproportionate amount of space in our minds yet ultimately boils down to just one small thing.

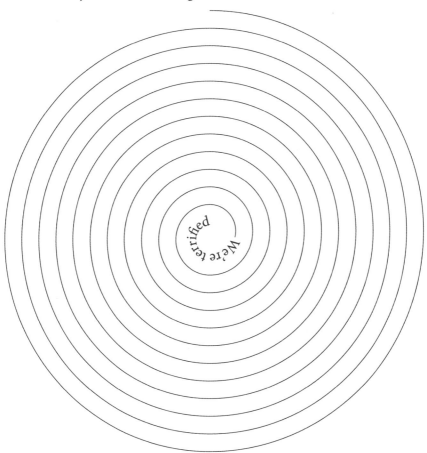

Yes, we are really scared, and we're right to feel terrified. The obstacles we are facing are appalling. Yet there are two different positions we can adopt:

A: I really want X + I'm terrified + it's theoretically possible
B: I don't really want X + it's not possible

A is the richer, more honest and raw psychological position. We are not reinventing our values and our desires to fit in with what is convenient.

We're admitting to our real aspirations even if they are painful and perhaps beyond our strength to realise.

Let's turn for a moment to the 20th-century French philosopher Jean-Paul Sartre. Sartre's most famous book, *Being and Nothingness*, was published in 1943.

In it, Sartre made a startling claim that underpins Existentialism, the philosophy which he pioneered: *that we are all fundamentally free.*

We constantly tell ourselves that we are not free in order to avoid feeling what Sartre called *angoisse* or 'anguish'. We comfort ourselves with necessities. We tell ourselves: 'I have to be in this marriage,' 'I have to live in this place,' 'I have to be in this boring job …'

Sartre gave a term to the phenomenon of living without taking freedom properly on board; it's what he called 'bad faith'. The most famous description of 'bad faith' comes in the middle of *Being and Nothingness*, when Sartre talks about a

Jean-Paul Sartre, c. 1959.
We are all fundamentally free.

waiter he knows, who gives off an impression that he simply could never be anything other than a waiter. He is unhappy but insists that what he is is all he can ever be. He pretends, says Sartre, to be first and foremost a waiter rather than a free human being.

Realising one's freedom in an existential sense should not be confused with a naïve self-help idea that we're all free to be or do anything without suffering pain or sacrifice. Sartre is far gloomier and more tragic than this. He merely wants to point out that we have more options than we normally believe.

Jean-Paul Sartre exercise

'If I could not fail, this is what I would do next …'

....

....

....

....

....

....

....

Write down one evolutionary step you promise you're going to take in the coming days in order to start the move towards becoming who you are. It might be as small as working through a few chapters of this book; or it might be about daring, at last, to have a certain sort of conversation with a boss or a partner.

....

....

....

....

....

....

....

We deserve to ensure that this book is only the beginning of a deep investigation into becoming who we really are.

16.
The Terror of a 'No'

There are many things we want to ask of other people around work. We want to ask for a job, for money, for a chance to collaborate, for an opportunity to talk to them. But we don't ask, because of the terror of a 'no'.

Why is a *no* – a tiny word with just two letters in it – so painful, so hard to hear, so much something we want to avoid, something we might even prefer to die in penury and loneliness rather than hear?

It's because when we hear 'no', we're not just hearing 'no'. We're hearing something far more hurtful and far more worrying. We're being brought face to face with what we can call the 'disgusting self'.

All of us have an 'acceptable self' and a 'disgusting self' inside our minds. Here are some of the adjectives that accompany the acceptable and disgusting selves respectively:

Acceptable self	Disgusting self
Dignified	Needy
Reserved	Desperate
Serious	Pathetic
Strong	Weird
Respectable	Ridiculous

What often happens when we hear a 'no' is that the disgusting self is activated and we start to hear not merely 'no' but also: 'No, you needy, desperate, pathetic, weird and ridiculous person.'

What we are hearing at such underconfident moments is entirely unwarranted – and a figment of our very lively and self-destructive minds. To get a sense of this, we only need to refer back to how we felt about people we rejected. We didn't generally hate them at all.

List some occasions when you heard a 'no':	What did they say exactly?	What did you hear? (Spot the difference …)

It's crucial to remember that other people do not have access to our disgusting self; we haven't shown it to them, and they don't know about it. The disgusting self is our own business – dating back, as ever, to certain unfortunate things in our distant past. So, we need to be careful not to import the verdict of the disgusting self into a situation where it doesn't belong.

When they say …	… they don't mean
'You're not fully qualified for the job.'	'You're a cretinous, arrogant buffoon who will never get anywhere with your sad, desperate life.'
'I've got a partner already.'	'You sicken me with your neediness and physical and mental degeneracy. The thought of being touched by you brings nausea.'
'No'.	'I despise you.'

In other words, we need to alter what we hear when we hear 'no'.

The number one reason why people say no to us – a reason that we are now going to frame in deliberately non-dramatic, non-personal, non-hysterical ways – is this:

It doesn't fit in with their plans.

When they say 'no', they are not thinking of:

- your stupidest deeds
- the nicknames people called you at school
- the slightly revolting and embarrassing things you sometimes do

These things are in your head, not theirs. We need to learn to isolate the meaning of 'no' from all the associations of your disgusting self.

There are two other things to bear in mind about the fearsome 'no'.

Firstly: we can survive a 'no'. Our associations around how survivable a 'no' is were frequently formed long ago, when we genuinely lacked both the inner resources and the outer freedom to deal very easily with a 'no'. In how we receive a dismissal, we may be falling back on patterns from early childhood. We need to remind our listening selves that things have moved on. We are eminently equipped to survive a 'no'.

Secondly: we don't ask for things, both because we're afraid to hear 'no' and also because we assume that the answer is going to be a no. But this will not always be the case.

Write down some surprisingly large things you would be open to giving, sharing or doing for someone else, *if they dared to ask*. (For example: an internship, some money, some time, a kiss ...)

....

....

....

....

....

....

....

....

....

....

....

....

....

We're often very determined to expect rejection. Because hoping is painful. Hoping would mean having to risk our dignity. But, in truth, we are fundamentally ignorant of others' plans. We can't really tell what they might say yes or no to. We just don't have access to their projects and vision.

We are attempting to overcome our lack of data in a pessimistic direction. We should, instead, try to get more data – by asking.

17.
Impostor Syndrome

In many challenges – personal and professional – we are held back by the crippling thought that people like us could not possibly triumph given what we know of ourselves: how reliably stupid, anxious, gauche, crude, vulgar and dull we really are. We leave the possibility of success to others, because we don't seem to ourselves to be anything like the sort of people we see lauded around us.

The root cause of impostor syndrome is a hugely unhelpful picture of what other people are really like. We feel like impostors not because we are uniquely flawed, but because we fail to imagine how deeply flawed everyone else must necessarily also be beneath a more or less polished surface.

Impostor syndrome has its roots in a basic feature of the human condition. We know ourselves from the inside, but others only from the outside. We're constantly aware of all our anxieties, doubts and idiocies from within. Yet all we know of others is what they happen to show and tell us: a far narrower, and more edited, source of information.

The solution to impostor syndrome lies in making a crucial leap of faith: that everyone must (despite a lack of reliable evidence) be as anxious, uncertain and wayward as we are. The leap means that whenever we encounter a stranger we're not really encountering a stranger; we're in fact encountering someone who is – in spite of the surface evidence to the contrary – in basic ways very much like us. Therefore, nothing fundamental stands between us and the possibility of responsibility, success and fulfilment.

The 16th-century French philosopher Michel de Montaigne once remarked, 'Kings and philosophers shit, and so do ladies.' He might have added, 'And so do top CEOs, entrepreneurs and creatives.'

1. Think of someone you think has made it in their career and – perhaps without focusing on the bathroom – construct a list of utterly humdrum, silly or (to them) exasperating things that could well come their way. We suggest kicking off with things like grating their fingers while grating Parmesan cheese, or having their children hide their car keys …

2. Mostly, others don't see your fears, though you have them. Turn this fact around: consider someone you normally see as having their life beautifully sorted out. Now imagine it's 3 a.m. and they are unable to sleep. What are the many painful thoughts that could be going through their mind? You don't know for certain, but you are correcting an imagination deficit.

3. We sometimes wait to be given 'permission' before we try something. We wait
    – that is – for someone else to tell us it's OK to do something (on occasion
    we call it 'encouragement', but the key point is that we're reliant on another
    for confidence).

    Imagine someone who doesn't ask for permission but just goes ahead with
    what they believe in; for them, really wanting to try something is enough
    reason to give it a go. If that mentality could be yours, what would you try?

18.
Why Now?

Career 'crises' tend to befall us at particular times, for reasons that we don't necessarily entirely understand but should study with generous attention. However valid it might be to examine the specifics of our career conundrums, it's also worth stepping back a little to ask why dissatisfaction might have descended at this particular juncture. Out of a desire to shield ourselves from challenging or anxiety-provoking truths, we might inadvertently be hiding some of the true causes of our mental distress.

For example, we might find it easier to say that we hate our job in general rather than to admit that we are being dragged down by a frostiness that has descended in our relationship with a particular colleague who we had once very much hoped to connect with. A powerful longing to find a new professional identity might – in a circuitous way – be bound up with unhappiness in our sex lives or sadness that our children are going to leave home soon.

This isn't to say that there's nothing wrong with our working lives, but simply to emphasise that we need to be as clear as possible about what exactly the problems might be, so as to ensure that we can accurately focus on the root causes of our restlessness.

In career therapy sessions, 'Why now?' is one of the most powerful questions ever raised, and we should keep our minds open to the many available answers. We might be in some sort of crisis but – with beautiful strangeness – perhaps not exactly the sort of career crisis we had initially imagined.

The potential insight is that our work may be the proxy target for another, less easily avowed distress. We're unhappy about something and work presents itself for blame because it's such a big factor in existence. And yet, as we analyse our distress, the real issues may be elsewhere. It's not such a strange phenomenon really. We shoot the messenger, we turn on the bystander. That's how our minds work: we turn on the nearest big thing, rather than address the real, hidden cause of our pain. By parsing our sorrows, we can reduce the collateral damage. Work, in fact, may be OK – it's something else that is causing us to feel unhappy about our lives.

What is unique to this moment?

Is there anything else distinctly challenging that might be unfolding?

If you could address something in your life other than your career, what might this be?

What's changed since you were last professionally content?

19.
Urgency

We often suffer not just from a desire to move jobs, but from a panicked sense that we need to move *right now*, even when, objectively, there is no immediate financial or practical necessity to do so.

The mind comes to a view that by taking a particular course of action, by 'doing something now', we will rid ourselves of what feels like an underlying agony or claustrophobia. We should notice the extent to which we are motivated not by a relaxed curiosity about another professional world, but by a desire to stop an inner suffering and restlessness.

This should give us pause for thought. Career therapy is, as a rule, suspicious of haste. It isn't that we never need to make a change. It's just that the longing to make a change while feeling that one has no alternative but to do so is often a sign that we're trying to solve a problem by deploying an only partially related solution. The time to move is when not moving might also – somehow – be an option.

If we can stay patient, we may realise that there is, in the background, an unconscious hope that a career move is going to spare us some kind of emotional toll: an ongoing humiliation, a feeling of not being valued, a sense of helplessness or unlovability. It might be that we need to go back and mourn something that went wrong in the past, rather than alter our job in the present.

Career therapists often operate with a curious rule of thumb: if it looks like a work problem, it may well, deep down, be a love problem. And, correspondingly, if it looks like a love problem, it can – oddly – turn out to be in essence a work problem.

How do you hope you will feel after this career move?

How do you think you will feel if you don't change?

What would be the dangers of not acting?

What are the dangers of gradual change?

Might it be a love problem rather than a work problem?

The stranger-sounding wisdom might be to do nothing until the dust settles. We're used to hearing advice in terms of radical moves, but in reality we are such complex beings that we may easily misdiagnose ourselves. Perhaps we need to rethink our career – only not now, but as something to be accomplished tomorrow. There's a legitimate intimate triage to be done: some problems we need to address today and others that can wait until tomorrow, or next year. There's only so much a career evolution can achieve. It won't change, perhaps, a relationship to a partner or a child; it may not address other, deeper courses of existential dread. So, we shouldn't rush to change our career as the imagined solution.

In addition, we need to think about our career in the long term: unless work is literally unbearable, we can (in the best sense) procrastinate. We can try to recognise the deeper love-problems first, before we sign an intemperate letter of resignation.

20.
The Agony of Choice

A lot of the reason why we don't move forward in our careers is that we are terrified of choice – and because, implicitly, we believe that there might be such a thing as a cost-free, perfect choice and, by extension, a flawless life.

To liberate ourselves to move forward, we should accept – with robust courage – the inevitability of pain around choice. The difficulty of choosing can mean that many of us spend our lives avoiding hard choices, which ends up being a kind of choice all of its own. But there is no alternative to picking something and to making our peace with the compromise that every choice entails.

We procrastinate, at times, in a desperate attempt to keep at bay the cruel limitations of reality. If we move to a new city, we might have new work prospects, but we'll lose our current friends; if we devote ourselves to one specific career, other sides of our character will be neglected.

If we delay choosing, all options appear to stay alive, at least as possibilities. Yet that is a grave illusion. We should quell our procrastination by accepting that not choosing is in itself a choice and that every choice will necessarily mean missing out on something important.

We should get better and faster at making decisions, sure in the knowledge that every decision will be in its own way slightly wrong and somewhat sad – while also slightly right and somewhat good.

Think about the upsides and downsides of making a career move

The upsides of moving jobs

....

....

....

....

....

....

....

The downsides of moving jobs

....

....

....

....

....

....

....

The upsides of staying put

....

....

....

....

....

....

....

The downsides of staying put

....

....

....

....

....

....

....

As you can see, there is no cost-free choice …

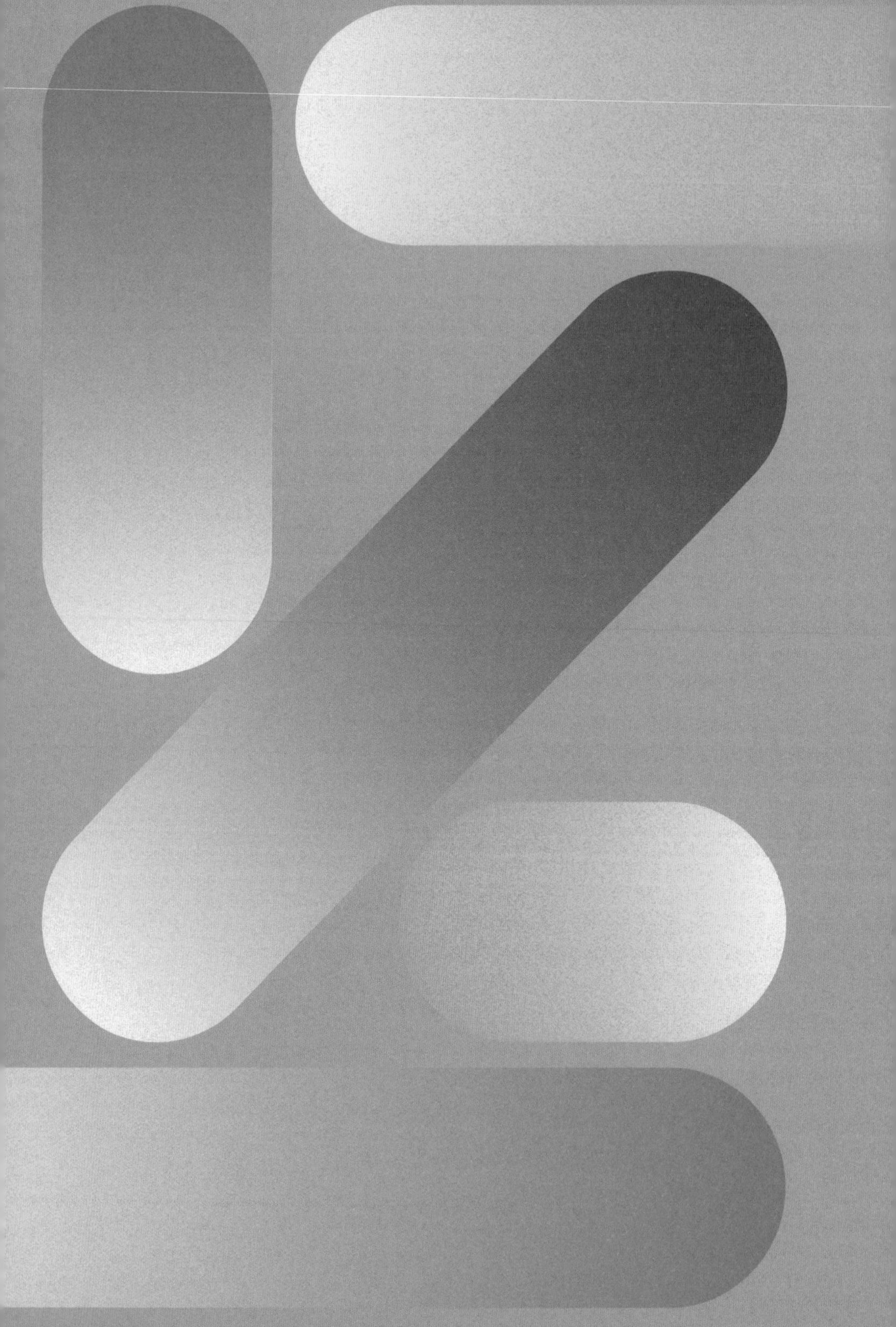

21.
A Future Self

Our imaginations tend to be so daunted by the practicalities required for us to change our lives that we grow inhibited about properly visualising the future that we ostensibly seek. We're so concerned with the next three moves we might make (and all the challenges involved in, say, a resignation, a return to education, etc. ...) that we don't richly explore what our lives might actually look like if everything worked out as we currently hope.

So, we should undertake a thought exercise in which we leap ahead ten years from now and picture our plans having come to fruition. We should evoke for ourselves both the broad outline of our lives and a range of specific details. We should think about what a typical Tuesday afternoon might look like and how it would be to contemplate a new week from the perspective of a Sunday evening. We might discover a host of complex and accurate pleasures, or, surprisingly, a selection of unexpected irritants and rather testing compromises.

Dreaming of the future in a frictionless way lends us the energy to look past the hurdles immediately before us, as well as, sometimes, granting us permission to remain exactly where we are.

Fantasy-longing is one of the most basic of all human pastimes. We paint for ourselves an impossibly idealised and utterly delightful picture of the future. Fantasy becomes our enemy: it tells us all the time about what we'd love but can never possibly have. The following questions are a refinement on the theme. Instead of asking our imagination to construct heaven on earth, we're turning our capacity for envisaging the future to a subtly – but importantly – different task: we're asking what, beautifully but realistically, our lives might be like.

Journey forward ten years: everything has worked out according to your current plans

How does your life feel?

....

....

....

....

How is an average week filled? What are you doing on a Thursday morning?

Mon	Tue	Wed	Thu	Fri	Sat	Sun

What pleases you?

....

....

....

....

What still annoys you?

....

....

....

....

We're making the extraordinary intellectual and emotional move of allowing a degree of realism to enter our daydreams. We're letting the normally hostile parts of ourselves enter into conversation: the optimistic, yearning part that wants everything to be lovely and the pessimistic part that knows that the troubles of life are never over. Can our pessimism and yearning find some middle ground in which they both have a voice, describing a future that's both possible and better?

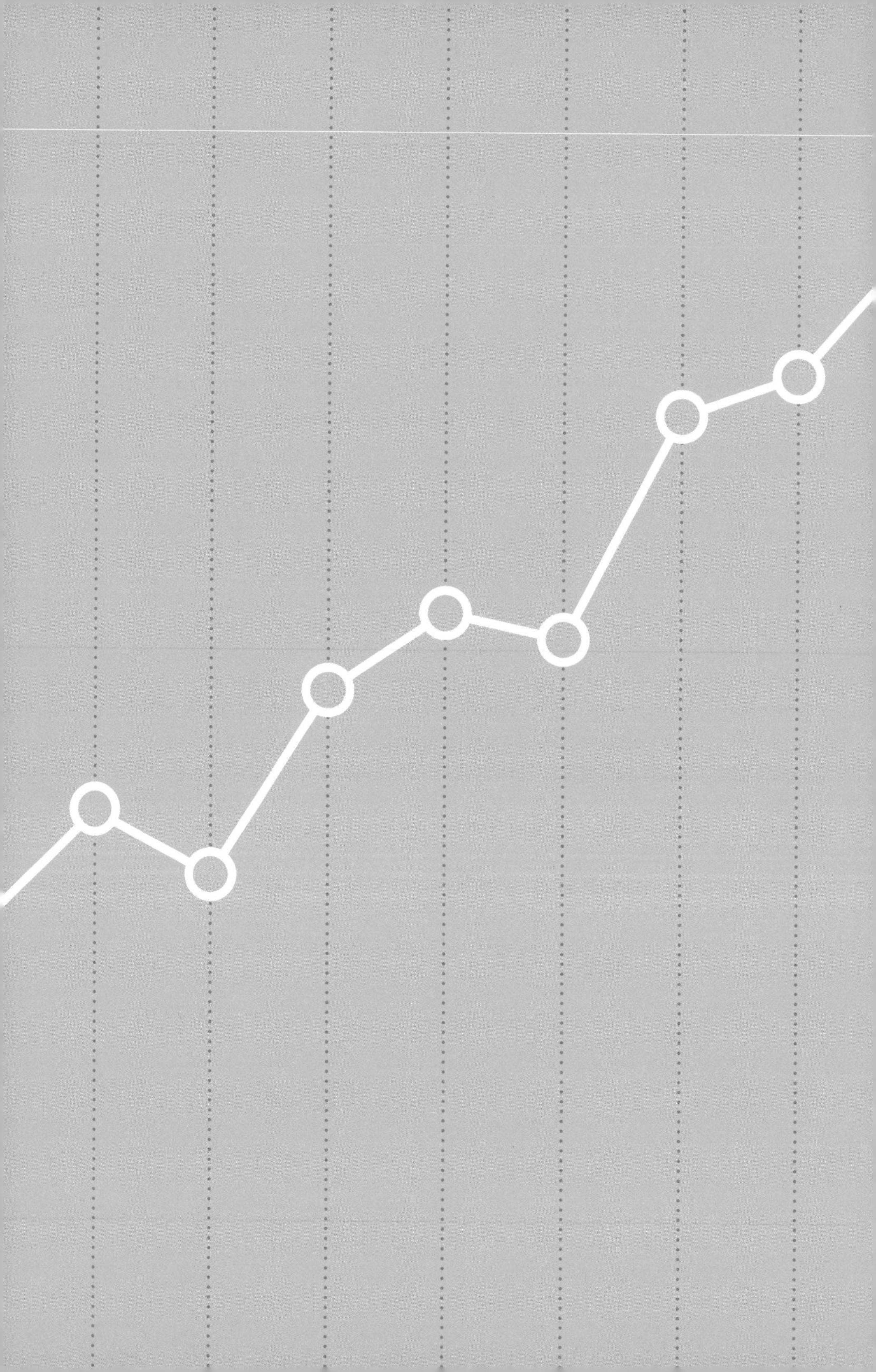

22.
Success

Surprisingly, perhaps, our desire to make a change in our career is frequently driven by having already succeeded well enough in some area or another – but then perhaps having grown bored or dissatisfied on discovering that success was not quite what we imagined it might be.

Before we move on too swiftly and pick yet another area to do well in, we should interrogate some of our underlying hopes about what success in any field can bring us.

We are used to framing our career ambitions in relatively practical terms: we speak of wanting money or fame, excitement or intellectual stimulation. But our true wishes can be fascinatingly emotional in nature. We should ask ourselves about the psychological benefits that we hope to secure through succeeding at our newest ambition. Our answers may feel strikingly odd, almost naïve or in some way quite disconnected from the job we're ostensibly trying to master. We might say that, if we succeed, we hope we will: 'finally be loved', 'no longer have to worry', or 'be able to make it up to everyone.'

Success is hard enough to secure: we should ensure that, if it were one day to be ours, it would truly offer us what we crave.

Without thinking too much, complete the following sentences

If I succeed, I will finally be able to ...

....

....

....

....

If my career goes as I want it to, I won't have to ...

....

....

....

....

Success to date has not quite brought me ...

....

....

....

....

It would be perplexing or sad if my future success couldn't deliver ...

....

....

....

....

We're trying to refine our picture of success. There are fantasy objectives that can never be real; however much we want to believe it, there's no way career triumphs can translate seamlessly into our wider hopes. Children absolutely do not love a parent more for them becoming vice president of marketing strategies; we don't develop more intimate friendships because our chain of bakeries is expanding; we may have won an industry accolade and still be no one in the eyes of our partner's friends.

The strange, deep truth is that career success, however brilliant, doesn't translate into simple, psychological appreciation and closeness. From a near perspective, we are never loved or admired for our outward accomplishments. We are always judged on what we are like in the present moment: are we sympathetic, sweet-natured, warm, good-humoured, gently candid or willing to see our own absurdity? Career success can bring many things, but not the free, tender love of others.

23.
After the Lottery

We operate in societies where the vast majority of people tell themselves that they work for one reason and one reason only: money. This may sometimes be true, but it's rare for anyone to work for cash alone, and the sensible-sounding nature of this motivation tends to mask a variety of other more fascinating and emotional motives we harbour for making it to work every day.

Before making any radical moves, we should ask ourselves what we might do if we won the lottery.

The question can evoke how much we lean on work for more than merely financial support. We do so, perhaps, to stave off anxieties about our legitimacy or ward off our fears of loneliness or worthlessness. Work might be compensating for intractable difficulties in our relationships or lending us opportunities to feel wanted and important. We might be trying, all the while, to repair a broken bond with a long-dead father or to impress an indifferent and narcissistic mother.

None of these ambitions are illegitimate. It's just that by insisting too much that we are simply financially driven, money-maximising creatures and are going to work because we 'need to', we miss out on understanding the complex psychological pleasures and compulsions that come from engaging with work – and we are therefore often not as accurate as we might be when choosing what task to devote ourselves to next.

The notion of an 'ingredient' is quite useful for analysing what, in our eyes, makes for a good job. Money may be a necessary ingredient – just as rice is a necessary ingredient for risotto – but it is not the only one. Work is such a big part of existence that it would, in fact, be a great pity if it yielded no benefits other than an income.

List five reasons why you work	Rank them in order of importance
1.	
....	....
2.	
....	....
3.	
....	....
4.	
....	....
5.	
....	....

What would you do after winning the lottery? How does this differ from what you're doing now?

....

....

....

....

What do you need work for, other than money?

....

....

....

....

24.
The Duty Trap

Every education system rewards duty and tends to encourage us to forget our true desires. After years of school and university, we often can't conceive of asking ourselves too vigorously what we might in our hearts want to do with our lives; what it might be fun to do with the years that remain. It's not the way we've learnt to think. The rule of duty has been the governing ideology for 80 per cent of our time on earth – and it's become our second nature. We are convinced that a good job is meant to be substantially dull, irksome and annoying. Why else would someone pay us to do it?

This dutiful way of thinking has high prestige, because it sounds like a road to safety in a competitive and alarmingly expensive world. But in fact, success in the modern economy will generally only go to those who can bring extraordinary dedication and imagination to their labours – and this is only possible when one is, to a large extent, having fun. Work produced merely out of duty is limp and lacking next to that done out of love. In other words, pleasure isn't the opposite of work; it's a key ingredient of successful work.

Yet we have to recognise that asking ourselves what we might really want to do (without any immediate or primary consideration for money or reputation) goes against our every, educationally embedded assumption about what could possibly keep us safe – and is therefore rather scary. It takes immense insight and maturity to remember that we will best serve others, and can make our own greatest contribution to society, when we bring the most imaginative and most authentically personal sides of our nature into our work. Duty can guarantee us a basic income. Only sincere, pleasure-led work can generate sizeable success.

Who taught you about duty?

Did following duty work for them?

Think of those you most admire: in what ways did they not follow duty?

What would be the satisfying but undutiful thing for you to do?

It can be quite a jolt to recognise that 'doing what we are supposed to do' may not actually be a very good script for us. But the duty map wasn't made by people who knew our needs or cared about us as individuals. To set duty to one side isn't instantly to become a renegade outsider.

To put it rather grandly, we're battling against a confusion that stems from the 18th-century Enlightenment. Duty – at that time – was what we accepted we had to do even though we may not necessarily have wanted to. Duty is at its peak when it goes against our inclinations. But this is a very bad theory of motivation. We're actually at our most useful when we like what we're doing.

By harnessing our work-pleasures, we may become more effective, more productive, more interested in responsibility and more devoted to customer satisfaction. We become better at work the more we can find work we enjoy.

25.
The Good Child

Many of us are good boys or girls. When we were little, we did our homework on time. We kept our rooms tidy. We wanted to help our parents. People imagine that good children are fine, because they do everything that is expected of them. And that, of course, is precisely the problem. The secret sorrows – and future difficulties – of the good boy or girl begin with their inner need for excessive compliance. The good child isn't good because by a quirk of nature they simply have no inclination to be anything else. They are good because they have no other option. Their goodness is a necessity rather than a choice.

Many good children are good out of love of a depressed, harassed parent who makes it clear they just couldn't cope with any more complications or difficulties. Or maybe they are very good to soothe a violently angry parent who could become catastrophically frightening at any sign of less than perfect conduct. But this repression of more challenging emotions, though it produces short-term pleasant obedience, stores up a huge amount of difficulty in later life.

Following the rules won't get you far enough. Almost everything that's interesting, worth doing or important will meet with a degree of opposition. A good child is condemned to career mediocrity and sterile people-pleasing.

The desire to be good is one of the loveliest things in the world, but in order to have a genuinely good life, we may sometimes need to be (by the standards of the good child) fruitfully and bravely bad.

How did you grow up 'good'?

What has being 'good' made you miss out on?

What would be the most interestingly rebellious thing you might do?

What was the 'good' child in you made to feel scared of?

The idea of being rebellious can sound deeply scary. We associate it, perhaps, with wasters, dropouts and people who never really find their feet in the world. But the model of rebellion needn't be Che Guevara on a motorbike. It could be a calm, rational figure like Thomas Jefferson or Florence Nightingale: people who recognised that the current order of the world was far from reasonable and that pliantly fitting in and 'being good' meant missing huge chances for sane and entirely practical improvement. We want to be 'naughty' not out of impish waywardness, but because the people who, fatefully, impressed us with the idea of conformity were, in fact, much less wise than we once assumed.

26.
Permission

When we were small, we needed permission to do pretty much anything at all – and the move was sensible. Others knew better than we did what was safe, what was socially acceptable, what would work, what was in line with our needs …

But for too many of us, this sensible childhood dynamic continues deep into the adult world, where it no longer serves any real purpose. We often know exactly what job we'd like to do next and are right in our hunches; and yet we remain stuck because we need someone else to give us permission to make the move that would render us happy.

Our block provides an occasion to reflect on an inhibition that must follow us through a number of situations in our lives. Somehow we are lacking trust, not in our abilities or our enthusiasms, but in our right to make big, positive decisions (perhaps about who to marry, how long to stay with a partner, where to live or how to work …). Instead, we naturally assume that there is someone out there, a parent or parental figure, who first has to wave us through or, alternatively, can say a definitive 'No'.

It's often with such feelings in mind that people finally visit a career therapist; they don't want advice, they simply (and just as importantly) crave permission.

We should, going forward, learn to give ourselves this permission, understanding how little trust was (probably) once placed in us in childhood by big people who called the shots. We should mourn the lack of agency that the past has bequeathed us – and take active steps to compensate for this vulnerability in the present.

We still need permission, of course, but it's a permission that can handily be sought from one person who counts above all else and is always to hand: ourselves.

Giving ourselves permission

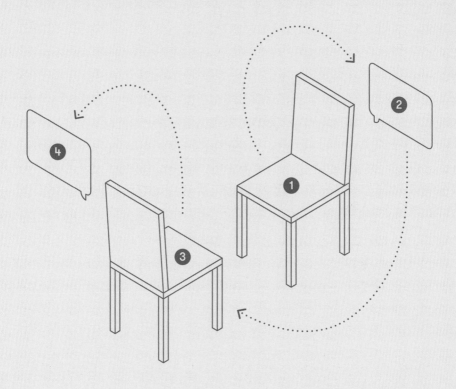

1. Place two chairs facing each other. Sit down in one of the chairs, facing the empty one, and imagine someone kind and caring and worldly sitting opposite you.

2. Tell them your hopes and fears, your wishes and your tribulations about moving on.

3. Then go and sit in the empty chair, facing your old chair and imagine speaking to you.

4. Now tell the chair opposite (you) that you have heard, that you understand and that you give them permission to act on their desires.

Reflect on the exercise; note in particular how you already have a 'voice' inside you that can give you permission in a kindly way. You just aren't used to seeking it out and listening to it. Do so from now on, whenever key decisions arise. Imagine a life in which you could more often, and more generously, give yourself permission.

27.
Self-affirmation

When we are in career difficulties, it is easy to get ever gloomier about our situation: we have failed, we lack talent, we don't have the required imagination or insight ...

Most of us have advanced degrees in self-destruction and self-suspicion. We may think that this gives us access to important truths about who we 'really' are. But in reality, hating oneself is no guide to any sort of truth and is merely a route to missed opportunities.

It's of course important to acknowledge our setbacks and our weaknesses, but never at the expense of caring for ourselves and appropriately celebrating what we're good at and can take pride in. After periods of critical introspection, there comes a moment when we need to shift course and accentuate the positives, to illustrate to ourselves how much we still have to offer. We should stop fearing that rejoicing at being us is always hubristic, arrogant or deluded. We should stop anticipating punishment if we get too overjoyed, or somehow fear that if we get one thing, something else might be taken away.

We should be aware of our tendency to say 'yes, but ...' and of how, when we want to take pride in an achievement, a cruel 'but' so often comes along to spoil our mood. 'I'm so happy I got this promotion, *but* it was sheer luck really.' 'I'm great at this job, *but* they must have hired me only because they knew about my dad ...'

We need to learn a very surprising lesson: that we are – despite a lot that we might have taken on board in childhood – in certain areas, genuinely rather wonderful.

For once, make the case for you. What are you rather brilliant or good at? What has gone well in your career?

....

....

....

Write down the top three achievements you feel really proud of, however large or small these may be.

1.
....

....

2.
....

....

3.
....

....

Imagine you were a good friend of yours: how would you sell 'you' to a prospective employer?

....

....

....

Learn to be a bit more suspicious of your innate modesty. Finish the sentence:

If I wasn't so modest, I might ...

....

....

....

To a nice person, it really does feel slightly impossible to 'big oneself up'; it feels like it must be pretence and egoism. But this is a genuine, difficult and serious form of self-knowledge; it's just oddly positive. The deep truth about who we are can't reasonably be all bad news. We accept that there are weaknesses we have that we shy away from admitting; the same logic implies that there might be slightly amazing things about who we are that we are equally disinclined to acknowledge.

Our world has fed us the image of the braggart – the idiot who can see only, often unreal, excellence in themselves, and we naturally recoil and want to do the opposite. But in recognising our merits, we're not aligning ourselves with the show-offs; we're completing an act of justice towards ourselves. We readily admit our areas of madness and absurdity and should, with corresponding candour, know what is fine and accomplished in our nature.

28.
The Status Quo

We live in a world that doesn't think very highly of people who don't move on. Career metaphors tend to have radical mobility built into them; it's all about paths and ladders, new horizons and bold trajectories.

This is often an extremely helpful stance (lending us courage and countering inbuilt timidity) but it can have an obtuseness of its own. There are situations when we may experience a genuine sense that we are not in the right job, and come to the view that moving on is the only option. We may share our intent with friends and colleagues, we may go into therapy, we may start to plan for a radical change for the rest of our lives and receive adulation from those around us for our courage and energy.

And then we may come to a rather embarrassing realisation: that having considered our options, our character, the real nature of our dissatisfaction and the impulses that drive us on, we'd rather stay put. We're OK where we are. We don't want to move at all. But of course, by now, this can seem extremely shameful, the coward's way out.

Far from it, we should accord as much prestige to a conscious decision to stay put as we do to a considered impulse to go elsewhere. There should be no shame in either direction.

Maybe our current position feels like a quiet resting place – but quiet resting places are fine. Maybe we'll never get to the top, but the middle has its legitimate attractions. Good, modest lives are an achievement in themselves. We shouldn't let others push us into a role that doesn't, on reflection, suit us, any more than we should let them prevent us doing something we genuinely want.

The status quo is not the enemy. It's simply another option, and often a very dignified and decent one at that.

Who would you be afraid of disappointing if you stayed put?

Who might be mean or judgemental towards you if you had a quiet life?

Where is the pressure to accelerate, increase, break barriers and rise to the next level coming from? Do you – on reflection – agree with it?

One side of you should now tell the other why a quiet life is, in fact, a hugely noble and valuable option.

In case you were wondering …

Our culture is desperately short of good, properly alluring images of the well-lived, modest life. This is perhaps almost inevitable: public acclaim would ruin the scenario. And yet we know it must be true: almost all good lives that have ever been lived have disappeared without a trace. We're psychologically fighting for our quiet, imperfect but real dignity against a society that measures the worth of a life in stupid ways. We're not bound to justify ourselves to *them* – only to ourselves.

29.
The Art of Confidence

A lot of the reasons why we end up in career difficulties can be traced back to a shortfall in confidence. It can be humbling to realise just how many great achievements haven't been the result of superior talent or technical know-how, merely that strange buoyancy of the soul we call confidence.

Let's start by trying to define what we mean by confidence. Here is some of what we have in mind:

- Confidence means being able to ask for what hasn't been offered.
- Confidence means not automatically and indiscriminately minding what everyone else thinks.
- Confidence means not overestimating others.
- Confidence means understanding how difficult everything worthwhile will be.
- Confidence means accepting one's own self-doubt, weakness and foolishness.
- Confidence means not interpreting rejection as a verdict on everything we are.
- Confidence means the faith that things can be changed for the better.

As societies, we tend to view whatever confidence level we have as fixed and inborn. We'll speak of some people as just confident and others as just unconfident – as if that were the end of the story.

But that's not what we at The School of Life think it is. We don't feel confidence is a *gift*. It is a *skill*. And that means it can be *learnt*.

You don't have to accept the level of confidence you currently have. You can grow more confident than you currently are – just as you can get fitter or better at French or the violin.

The traditional education system teaches us to be confident in a range of technical fields:

- how to fill out a spreadsheet
- how to write reports
- how to deliver a presentation …

But what is almost never taught is confidence itself, the essence of confidence that can be applied in any number of fields, from the very small to the very large:

- how to speak to strangers at parties
- how to ask someone for a raise
- how to ask someone where the toilet is
- how to change the world

We believe that confidence is ultimately about having certain confidence-inducing ideas in mind – and about keeping them at the forefront of our thoughts on a regular basis.

No baby lacks confidence – they scream with abandon. When did you learn to hold back on your demands?

....

....

....

....

....

Who crushed your confidence when you were little or (also) as an adolescent? Can you list the people who gave you the impression that you didn't deserve to be treated well?

What might you, benignly, think of these people today? (They might have hurt you because they were hurt themselves.)

What might be lovely about a stranger coming up to you at a party?

....

....

....

....

....

How would you react if a nice but nervous person asked you where the bathroom is?

....

....

....

....

....

How would you respond to someone who genuinely wanted your guidance?

....

....

....

....

....

At the root of so much lack of confidence in good people is a strange failure of symmetry. We know how warmly and gently we'd react to the awkwardness or shyness of others – and almost everyone is like us. But we've let a small minority of rather harsh people represent what we suppose 'others' are generally like. It's really rather tragic: we're letting the occasional worst triumph over the normally decent.

Confidence, it turns out, isn't grounded so much in belief in oneself as outstanding, but in the secure knowledge that only a very odd and troubled individual would go out of their way to deliberately distress another human being.

30.
Befriending the Inner Idiot

We're going to start by imagining a couple of situations where some of us would feel very underconfident.

- We're at a networking event where we'd very much like to go up to a colleague in our industry who it would be helpful to meet.
- We'd like to push forward a new idea at work but are terrified by what our team members might say.

At many moments of underconfidence, we're faced with two contrasting emotions: a *wish* and a *fear*.

The wish is to seem serious to others and most importantly to oneself, by which we mean:

- competent
- worldly
- adult
- self-contained
- elegant
- composed

And the fear is of seeming an idiot to oneself and others, by which we mean:

- needy
- frail
- disgusting
- eccentric
- weird
- a loser

The normal way that people suggest we become more confident is to try to resolve the oscillation in favour of the wish. They try to reassure us that we are – despite our fear – actually in reality serious, elegant, composed, etc. We are really not – these kindly people say – idiots.

This is very well-meaning and very kind. But we find it doesn't work, because it isn't fundamentally true – and it isn't the way we do things at The School of Life. Here we take a very different approach. Rather than saying that we are all serious, we like to make ourselves at peace with the thought that we are – in actual fact – all idiots. All of you, everyone out in the street, everyone in the government, in fact, everyone everywhere pretty much at every moment.

Complete the following list

Despite how I may disguise it, I'm seriously idiotic in (at least) the following five big ways:

1.
....
....

2.
....
....

3.
....
....

4.
....
....

5.
....

Think of a dear friend. Without being mean, where does their idiocy lie?

....
....
....

You know the oddest details about yourself, but how much of this would an average acquaintance really see? Reverse the proposition: how much of their own private madness would they be likely to let you see?

....
....
....
....

Seven billion idiots

All of us are blundering fools. We lie, we steal, we slander, we've got weird habits, we get up to funny stuff in the night, we bump into doors, we fart, we look ridiculous, we have odd thoughts and dreams … In short, we're totally daft. Strangely, this idea is very helpful for giving us confidence.

There's a type of underconfidence that arises specifically when we grow too attached to our own seriousness and become anxious in any situation that might show up our idiocy. We hold back from challenges in which there is any risk of ending up looking ridiculous – which comprises, of course, almost all the most interesting situations.

In a concerted bid never to look foolish, we don't venture very far from our cocoon, and thereby – from time to time, at least – we miss out on the best opportunities of our lives.

We imagine that it might be possible to place ourselves beyond idiocy. We trust that it is an option to lead a good life without regularly making a complete idiot out of ourselves. Instead, what we need to do is explicitly to befriend our inner idiot. We all have one. You know it's there. Mostly you're desperate to stay away from the inner idiot. But please don't. Make friends with it. Get to know it in broad daylight. And be assured that everyone else has an inner idiot too.

31.
Criticism

It is hard to achieve anything without encountering criticism. At some point, almost inevitably:

- someone will describe us as arrogant
- someone will describe us as wrong
- someone will hold a negative view of us

The question is what happens next.

Certain people seem able to take criticism in their stride. It doesn't rattle their confidence or their sense of self. They still like and believe in themselves. Others are entirely devastated by it; they automatically panic and start to lose faith in who they are.

So, we fall into two camps in relation to criticism:

1. 'I need the approval of the world to feel OK about myself.'
2. 'I don't need the approval of the world to feel OK about myself.'

To be able to feel OK without the approval of the world hugely increases our feeling of confidence when we run into criticism. Whereas to be immediately unnerved by opposition turns us into people-pleasers – those who have no option but to prioritise the ideas of others over their own.

What explains confidence or the lack of it? It all has to do with the sort of love we tasted in childhood.

The feeling that we don't need the approval of the world to be OK is almost always a sign of having enjoyed the strong approval of a few people very early on in our lives. Whereas the feeling that we constantly need the approval of the world to be OK is normally a sign of having not enjoyed the strong approval of a few people very early on in our lives.

In other words, in our childhoods, we can speak of there being two kinds of parental love that we might have been the beneficiaries of: the extrinsic and the intrinsic varieties. These two varieties of love are associated with very different beliefs, which we have put into a table here.

Two varieties of parental love

Extrinsic love	Intrinsic love
'Other people' are generally right	'Other people' can well be wrong
Famous and prestigious institutions are usually right	Famous and prestigious institutions can be wrong
Being applauded by the world makes you more love-worthy	Being applauded by the world makes you no more love-worthy
Being condemned by the world makes you less love-worthy	Being condemned by the world makes you no less love-worthy

Do you feel yourself to have been more, on balance, the beneficiary of extrinsic love? Or the beneficiary of intrinsic love?

....

....

....

....

....

How has this shaped your level of confidence as you have gone through adult life?

....

....

....

....

....

The question now is what we can do if we have not enjoyed intrinsic love. The solution is as follows.

Firstly, we need to recognise what has happened; we need to acknowledge that we have something lacking in us and mourn its loss. We missed out on having to hand an intrinsic love that would have been extremely helpful to us in negotiating adult life.

Secondly, we need to learn to give ourselves the intrinsic love that no one else gave us early on. We have to model an ideal intrinsic voice of love and speak to ourselves in it.

It shouldn't sound too weird to suggest that we can learn to model an inner voice and speak to ourselves in it. This is exactly what Catholicism urges people to do in relation to Jesus. We should, says the Church, learn about how Jesus spoke to other people – and then speak to ourselves in that voice in relation to our challenges. At moments of crisis, we can explicitly ask ourselves: 'What would Jesus say now?'

We need to do something similar, not with Jesus, but with a voice of intrinsic love: we need to learn to speak to ourselves in it reliably.

The good news is that we almost all know how to do this voice. It's the voice we speak to our friends in, when they're in trouble – but which we pointedly usually don't use with ourselves.

Try practicing the voice of intrinsic love. Model what this voice would say in relation to:

News that someone hates us

....

....

....

....

....

....

....

At The School of Life, we fancifully like to think that the voice of intrinsic love might sound a bit like Michel de Montaigne – a man who always stood out against public opinion, who is refreshingly his own person, who urges his readers to have faith in themselves, who celebrates simplicity and independence and writes things like:

I have seen in my time hundreds of craftsmen and ploughmen wiser and happier than university chancellors – and whom I'd rather be like.

So we might ask, at moments when criticism at the office is wearing us down: 'What would Montaigne say now?'

32.
How Long Is There Left?

Career change is frightening. So as to gain confidence, we should more often dwell on something even scarier: how soon we will be dead. Next to this ghastly idea, the slight discomfort of moving jobs or of retraining will – redemptively – be revealed as essentially trivial and easily mastered. We often behave as if we were immortal. Why else would we fail again and again to square up to what we need to do? We are not terrified enough for our own good. We are behaving like gods or superhuman entities who have centuries to get it right.

To overcome our tendencies to delay and evade, we need to bring the pressure of another – and even greater – fear to the situation. We need to scare ourselves with something very large in order to liberate ourselves to think with greater energy about the myriad of immediate challenges before us. Death should also liberate us somewhat not to mind too much if we do hit obstacles in more ambitious ventures, for if everything is in any case doomed to end in the grave, then it might not matter if we fail wholeheartedly. The thought of death may be at once terrifying and the harbinger of a distinct kind of light-heartedness and requisite irresponsibility.

Look up how long a person in your part of the world tends to live. Remember it is only an average. Imagine that the last decade or more can be spent not feeling at your best, and not at work.

You are told you have only one year left to live. What kind of job could you imagine having in which you'd want to work more, not less, in the remaining time?

....

....

....

....

....

Given how short life is, what jobs feel important despite our lack of time?

....

....

....

....

What do you want your impact on the world to have been?

....

....

....

....

To be frank about our own finitude is inherently difficult. The ideal is, of course, not to die soon but to live for a very long time as if time were running out. It's not the actual likelihood of imminent death we're invoking but the thought of it. And we won't just become braver and more focused; we might also become more generous, more forgiving, more tender and more sympathetic.

We are all poor, mortal creatures, destined to die and understandably desperate to reject this knowledge. It's strange that such painful thoughts can cause us to not simply despair but to dig deeper into our longings and ideals while there is still time.

33.
Readiness for Difficulty

There's a particular kind of crisis of confidence that occurs when we begin a project with great hope and energy, but then find ourselves hitting difficulties that we hadn't foreseen.

Quickly we can find that we lose confidence in ourselves and our abilities to get the project done, so we fall into despair and give up. This can happen in a variety of contexts:

- writing a novel
- running a profitable new business
- becoming a stand-up comedian
- painting pictures
- baking artichoke and courgette soufflé

When we try to understand our failure, we readily say that we gave up because the task was hard. But that isn't exactly true; in reality, we gave up because the task was hard *and harder than we expected it to be.*

The issue of expectation is central to understanding losses of confidence and overcoming them. One of the big problems of individual and collective life is that we don't have sufficiently accurate ideas of how difficult things are. We don't actually know how hard it is to:

- run a business
- manage a relationship
- find a fulfilling career

We're constantly giving up on things because we have not been adequately prepared for the tasks ahead.

Why don't we have an accurate sense of the difficulties? There are a number of reasons. One of them is that our desire to achieve something is often sparked by being the *customer* of a particular product or service, rather than its *producer*. It's in the nature of being a customer that you are not fully told of the struggles of the producer, simply because it would destroy the product or service to divulge the effort going on behind the scenes. So, we meet the stark, haunting and pure paintings of Francis Bacon long before we might ever go into his studio – a place where the agonies of creating these silent masterpieces are symbolised by the chaos and jumble of painterly materials.

We tend to see the finished writings of the novelist, not the tortured confusion of the earlier drafts. We tend to eat a lot more tasty and beautifully presented things before we are taken – as it were – behind the scenes into the kitchen and start to learn of the challenges of cooking. As the Roman poet Horace said, to describe the way producers hide difficulties from consumers: 'Art lies in concealing the art.'

Francis Bacon, *Self-Portrait*, 1978

Francis Bacon's studio, London

But we pay a high price for having news of the struggle kept from us. There comes a point when we move from being consumers to being producers, and we suffer for our ignorance. We run into difficulties, which we interpret as a sign that we cannot succeed. We don't interpret our defeats correctly. We have not seen enough of the early drafts of those we admire – and therefore cannot forgive ourselves the hell of our own first attempts.

Here is a quick, fun quiz about the difficulties of achievement:

1. How many years did Marcel Proust have to write in obscurity until he was recognised?

2. How old was the architect Zaha Hadid before she got to build something in her own adopted country, the UK?

3. How many publishers turned down George Orwell's *Animal Farm*?

4. How many hours of practice are required to become a professional violinist?

There's a nice quote on this from the philosopher, Friedrich Nietzsche:

*The recipe for becoming great is easy, but it's a lot easier to say:
'I do not have enough talent.' Do not speak of inborn talent, of innate
giftedness. We can only ever be as great as our appetite for suffering.*

Part of the reason we weren't correctly prepared for suffering has to do
with our childhoods. The difficulty of life is often hidden from children
by otherwise kindly parents. These parents do not tell us difficult truths,
including:

- how difficult it is to bring up a family
- how demoralising work can be
- how appalling it is to get old
- how perplexing relationships always are

Instead, they read to us about the adventures of Miffy, the adorable bunny.
And they think they are helping us.

Dick Bruna, *Miffy*, 1979

Setbacks shouldn't make us lose confidence. They should reassure us that
life is proceeding exactly according to plan.

Confidence isn't the belief that we won't meet obstacles. It is the
recognition that hellish difficulties are an inevitable part of any worthwhile
achievement.

What did your upbringing teach you might be easier than it actually is?

....

....

....

....

....

....

....

....

What do you feel motivated this wrong picture?

....

....

....

....

....

....

....

....

34.
Processing the Past

One thing that's liable to get missed when we move jobs is the tricky truth that we ultimately had to change course because, in one way or another, *something went wrong*. Perhaps we misjudged what our real ambitions were; we failed to get on with colleagues; we fell afoul of office politics; we realised that our temperament wasn't welcome … Something sad and bad brought us to alter the course of our lives.

Amidst the excitement of change, we tend to forget the uncomfortable past and focus instead on the next job and all that it can bring us. But in the process, we are in danger of missing out on valuable information – and of not sufficiently sifting through the unhappy evidence thrown up by our recent experiences. We need to take time to ponder our setbacks or dead ends. We can't reliably build a happy future without understanding in detail what didn't work out before now. There are important truths about ourselves and our weaker or more complicated sides lurking within the story of our old job. It isn't inevitably someone else's fault. It wasn't just a rubbish company. It's too simple to say we 'simply wanted a change'. All these sound like attempts to bypass a vital confrontation with regret, ambivalence and mishap.

We should allow ourselves to be self-reflective, frustrated and a little sad. There was probably some kind of anger that helped to drive us to make a change – and this needs to be given a proper airing. Without some form of emotional processing, we may get mildly depressed, as we do whenever something painful hasn't been properly understood and felt.

We have to ensure we have properly dissected and mourned the past before we have any right to be confident about our future plans.

It's a form of real courage to be honest about past disappointments. But we take encouragement from the fact that no modern person can ever live a perfect life. We're not hopeless because we messed up; we're just acknowledging a pretty much universal experience – the difference is that we're analysing it, rather than avoiding thinking about it. We can't escape our failures; the question is whether we can learn from them.

What were your initial hopes for your last job?

How did your last job disappoint you?

If there's anger somewhere in your feelings, what are you angry about?

How did others let you down?

How did you let yourself down?

What would you – with the benefit of hindsight – have done differently?

35.
Confidence in Confidence

Though we assume that we want to be confident, actually – in our hearts – we may harbour private suspicions about being confident. We may secretly remain attached to hesitancy, modesty and meekness.

It isn't always that we don't know how to be confident. We may not even really want to be confident. Let's not forget that, for many hundreds of years, Jesus loomed very large in the imagination of many societies. Christianity emphasised that being good means not pushing oneself forward, not fighting for more, not believing one is superior to anyone else. The meek shall inherit the earth. We may also have picked up some very negative associations about confidence from people we know, who were confident as well as being some pretty unpleasant other things.

Confidence can be associated with:

- shouting a lot
- being arrogant
- never backing down
- being mean

But, in fact, the truth is that being confident does not have to be connected to many of the negatives that frequently accompany it. Being confident can also be compatible with:

- being polite
- being modest
- backing down
- being gentle

We need to separate confidence from some of its negative associations. Some of the reason we may be suspicious of confidence is that most of us, in childhood, were very confident – bordering on egomaniacal – in some settings. We typically start off as egomaniacs as small children: it is (early on) entirely forgivable to feel we might be at the centre of the world.

As we grow, however, most of us learn very quickly that this behaviour is no longer acceptable and may actually get us in trouble. By our early teens, we start to get more modest – a pattern that can continue throughout life. Instead of seeking attention, we try to blend in: dressing like our friends in high school, behaving like our colleagues in our first job, buying houses and cars similar to those our friends have as we age. But we can go too far in this kind of modesty.

What bad experiences have you had around being confident?

....

....

....

....

....

....

Why might the idea of confidence be scary?

....

....

....

....

....

We should allow ourselves to develop confidence in confidence by thinking that we can be confident in our own way. We can avoid the bad models of confidence:

- the egomaniac
- the shouter
- the nasty person

We can be confident about remaining ourselves, just a slightly bolder and more courageous version of who we are right now.

36.
We Could Survive

One of the characteristic flaws of our minds is to exaggerate how fragile we might be; to assume that life would be impossible far earlier than it in fact would be. We imagine that we could not live without a certain kind of income or status or health; that it would be a disaster not to have a certain kind of relationship, house or job.

Adverts exaggerate this tendency. They go to extraordinary lengths to get us to feel that we really do need all kinds of luxury:

- to go skiing once a year
- to have heated car seats
- to fly in business class
- to own the same kind of watch as a famous actor
- to have perfect muscular health

In fact, our core needs are much simpler than all this. We could in fact manage perfectly well with very much less. Not just around possessions but across every aspect of our lives. It's not that we should *want* to: it's simply that we *could*.

We could cope quite well with being rather poor, not being very popular, not having a very long life and with living alone. We could even, to put the extreme instance forward, cope with dying; it happens all the time.

But we forget our resilience – and so grow more timid than we should. Our lives become dominated by a fear of losing things which we could (in fact) do perfectly well without.

The ancient Roman philosopher Seneca had great success running what we would now call a venture capital firm.

Seneca: how to practice
losing everything.

Seneca owned beautiful villas and magnificent furniture, but he made a habit of regularly sleeping on the floor of an outhouse, eating only stale bread and drinking lukewarm water. He did this to remind himself that it wouldn't be so bad to lose everything – and to free himself of nagging worries of catastrophe. The realisation gave him great confidence.

It would be better for our confidence if our society could stop presenting us with rags-to-riches stories, and if it instead presented us with far kinder and incidentally, far more confidence-inducing stories: riches-to-rags stories.

In the riches-to-rags stories, we'd meet people who lost money, partners and social standing but ended up coping really rather well with their new lives. Our culture would not be recommending such scenarios, just reducing the fear around them – so as to lend us confidence.

Devise a riches-to-rags story

Take a successful and famous person – an actor or musician, a politician or entrepreneur – and imagine their adjustment from fame and fortune to ordinary life. How might they cope, and indeed almost rather enjoy, their 'rags'-like life?

....

....

....

....

....

....

We shouldn't – of course – want disaster to strike us. But we can take confidence from the sure fact that we would know how to endure it if it came.

Now list what risky but rewarding venture you might plan?

....

....

....

....

....

....

....

How might you survive its failure? What does a minimal viable life look like?

....

....

....

....

....

....

How much money would you like?

....

....

....

....

....

....

How much could you actually live on?

....

....

....

....

....

....

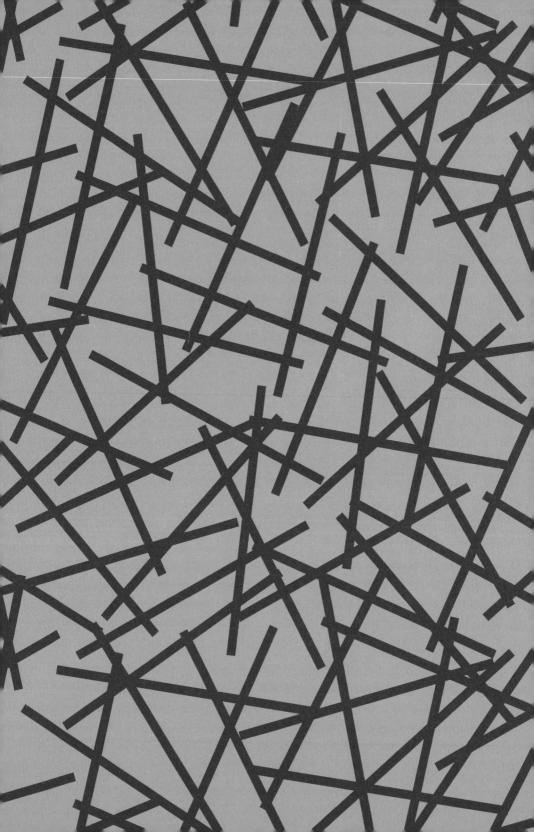

37.
I've Screwed Up

One of the greatest problems of our working lives is that we lack any experience of, or instruction in, the essential art of *failing well*. Because our efforts are focused on appearing utterly professional and flawless, because we are guided by an underlying and punishing notion that we might avoid failure altogether, we lack the energy or insight to respond productively to our inevitable stumbles. We forget an essential truth: the issue at work is never whether we will fail or not; simply whether we will fail *well* or not.

Our bad failures tend to follow a familiar pattern: we deny that anything has gone, or could even go, wrong. When conclusively rumbled, we deny there is much of an issue, blame the person who upbraids us, and suggest they might be being absurdly mean or critical. Or else we fold and go in for histrionic apology, beg for our lives, overdo the contrition and make our colleagues wish they had never said anything to begin with.

A wiser response to screwing up might have some of the following components:

1. A clear and unashamed sorry

I'm going to put my hands up here. I've made a mistake. I'm so sorry.

Half of the population at least is trapped in defensive-perfectionist patterns of behaviour. That is, they suffer from an extreme reluctance to acknowledge fault and when it's pointed out to them, imagine that their entire selves are under assault, as opposed to trusting that it is merely one of their behaviours that is being critiqued. They are told it would be great if they could increase the margin size on a document. All they can hear is 'You don't deserve to exist.' One tells them it would have been great if the August figures had been a bit higher; they assume you want them dead. A prerequisite of a good apology is therefore a sound sense of self. You can fail and still have every right to walk the earth.

2. A technical explanation for the screw up

One reason I messed up was because the systems I'm working with meant that …

There is almost always, at some level, a technical reason for an error. It pays for everyone to know what this might be – so that corrections can be put in place. This indicates that there is only one thing the senior management ever really cares about when it comes to mistakes: that things can get better going forward. There is complete disinterest in poring over the entrails of the failure – except in so far as this can help with the future. Our task is to draw attention to every clue that will help them in this regard.

3. An emotional explanation for the screw up

If I can be frank for a moment, there's a lot going on at home, which means I might not have been in the best frame of mind.

We too often enter the workforce with the punishing idea that to be a good employee means being an emotionless automaton, and therefore that having to admit to emotional disruptions is tantamount to declaring oneself unemployable. But our terror stems from a misunderstanding. The good-enough employee isn't the one who never endures some emotional static, it's the one who can get a perspective on their fragilities and can be honest about their difficulties from a background appreciation of their many genuine strengths.

4. Evidence of lessons drawn

What I'm going to take away from this incident is three things in particular. Firstly, ..., secondly ..., thirdly ...

Companies never set out to replace people; they want to develop the ones they have – and so what they crave is a hopeful narrative of why they should keep faith with those already in their posts. That means, in essence, that they long for employees to show what exactly they have learnt from each of their mistakes.

5. A capacity to move on

Now for the meeting next week ...

It's distinctly possible to apologise too much. If we plead for forgiveness, insist we are the world's greatest idiot or swear never to make the slightest mistake ever again, it suggests we don't have a clear sense of the reality of the situation. Our tears don't bring back lost profit and our promises sound untrue. The most useful thing we can do, to express our maturity and competence, is to get back to our desk, remain confident and work with ever greater astuteness.

We're never going to have a life in which we don't screw up, and no one has ever had an employee who never made a mistake. A problem can be real but not fatal. People can get annoyed while really being more interested in a solution than retribution. It's a huge step in our self-understanding to recognise ways in which we might be having difficulties with our own imperfections. The key to progress is imagining the situation, realistically, from the other side, where the person asking us to improve isn't a monster.

When you are criticised, does it tend to feel catastrophic? The interesting move is to try things the other way round. Suppose you want to say that someone has messed up in a particular way – how would you feel if they took it as a global assault on their existence?

....

....

....

....

....

....

....

Imagine someone at work is apologising to you. What do you really hope will happen in future and what could they say now that would reassure you?

....

....

....

....

....

....

....

....

Do you ever get cross with someone while, in the background, thinking they are basically OK?

....

....

....

....

....

....

....

Describe in as much detail as you can your own experience of feeling local exasperation and overall positivity. Then imagine someone else feeling that way about you.

....

....

....

....

....

....

....

....

38

Laying Down Boundaries

One of the reasons why our working lives might be less than they should be is that we have missed out on an awkward sounding but critical art (whose absence we may until now never even have noticed): that of *laying down boundaries*.

Laying down a boundary involves informing those around us – colleagues, parents, children, lovers – of a given set of objectively reasonable things that we are going to require in order to feel respected and happy, while doing so in a way that conveys confidence, self-possession, warmth and a mixture of kindness and strength.

Those who can successfully lay down boundaries will tell their small child that though they love them very much, in fact, once this game is over, Mummy or Daddy are not going to want to play another round and it will be time to go upstairs for hair washing and there's simply no other way, darling chipmunk, however disappointing I know this will sound and biting or kicking is not the answer, as we've discussed before. The good boundary-builder will wait until everyone is well rested to tell their partner that though they love them to take the initiative in a hundred areas, when it comes to their own family, they want to be left in charge – and therefore don't think it was right for the partner to call up their mother-in-law without warning in order to arrange the forthcoming holidays. And at work, the boundaried manager will tell their new hire that though they want to be supportive where possible, it simply isn't their role to complete schedules or manage budgets for others.

However, because most of us have not been educated in this byway of emotional maturity, the boundaries are either non-existent or else get thrown up in a jerky and destructive manner; as the technical language has it, we are either too compliant or too rigid. Mummy or Daddy might not, therefore, ever say they've had enough of the game and, even when wilting, will play on late into the night, ensuring that chipmunk will be exhausted and cross the next day, as well as craving the security that comes from knowing that their grown-up is 'grown up' enough to say no – even to what they ostensibly badly want (if there's one thing we crave more than that our wishes are granted, it's someone responsible enough to resist granting them all). In a relationship, we might never explain what we require in order to feel content and therefore either store up our resentments (and – usually – therefore grow unable to have sex) or else burst into unexplained rages that exhaust our partner's capacity for love. At work, meanwhile, we might develop a reputation as a friendly pushover or as an unreasonable tyrant whom it becomes a lot of fun to try to evade.

Those who can't lay down boundaries have invariably not, in their early lives, had their own boundaries respected. Someone didn't allow them to say when they were unhappy with a genuinely difficult situation; someone didn't give much of a damn about their hurt feelings or distinctive hopes. Someone insinuated that being good meant falling in line, always, immediately. No one modelled the skill of winning, graceful objection. And so now, when the time comes to make a request of others, three powerful anxieties bedevil the boundary-less person:

- If I speak up, they will hate me.
- If I speak up, I will become a target for retribution.
- If I speak up, I will feel like a horrible person.

Though such fears manifest themselves as unquestionable certainties, they are amenable to gentle probing. People almost never hate those who make polite and reasonably framed demands; in fact, they tend to respect and like them a little more. They feel in the presence of a maturity and kindly authoritativeness that appear worthy of their time, as well as seeming rare and a bit thrilling. Frustrating someone's wishes doesn't have to be evidence of selfishness, it may signal a noble concern for another's long-term well-being and flourishing. One can adore someone, wish them the very best, have the kindest intentions towards them and still, very diplomatically and yet very decisively, tell them no.

An alternative response to building boundaries is a habit of throwing up walls topped with razor wire ringed by machine gun turrets or, to put it more colloquially, a tendency to get swiftly and gratingly defensive. The manically defensive person is also labouring under a set of highly unfortunate misapprehensions:

- that everyone is trying to hurt them badly

- that no one will listen unless they hit back with immense force
- that their needs cannot ever truly be met

Yet the alternative to lacking all boundaries is not violent defensiveness. We should not let boundary-building be undermined by its most zealous practitioners; there is always a means to make a sound case without reaching for a weapon.

It takes a little self-confidence and courage to be able to notice just how bad we may be at the art of boundary-laying. We may have spent a large chunk of our lives already in an essentially passive relationship to everyday infringements by people close to us. But we aren't a piece of helpless flotsam on the river of others' wishes; we have agency, direction and – as it were – a rudder. The price to pay for affection isn't compliance. We can gradually take on board a highly implausible-sounding but redemptive notion: that we can prove loveable and worthy of respect and at the same time, when the occasion demands it, as it probably will a few times every day, utter a warm-sounding but definitive 'no'.

Where do you feel that you might be lacking boundaries at work?

....

....

....

....

....

....

What are you afraid of if you said 'no' more often?

....

....

....

....

....

....

What would you like to tell people going forward?

....

....

....

....

....

....

39.
Do It Now!

A deadline is looming, and a member of your team hasn't made much progress on the crucial part of the task that's been assigned to them. You feel like going up to them and insisting they make a concentrated effort immediately: *Do it now!* The strong temptation is to get stern and controlling – and keep them at it, under your eye if need be, until it's finished.

But there's a huge problem: your peremptory demands are very likely to undermine your colleague's ability to perform. They'll feel flustered and harassed; they'll not be able to muster the necessary levels of attention and energy; they'll make mistakes. Just as significantly, they'll get resentful: they'll begin to see you as a tyrant to be hated rather than a team member to be helped.

The more work requires the use of the mind, the more galling the situation becomes. It's possible (at a theoretical extreme) to make someone hew rocks or chop trees more or less at gunpoint. For thousands of years, the only tool of management was the whip. But it's not nowadays remotely possible to motivate an unhappy employee to identify an anomaly in the year-end accounts or come up with a resonant ad slogan or make an elegant refinement to a dress design by being mean and impatient. The more worried, oppressed or anxious an individual feels, the less likely it is that the creative and delicate elements of their mind will ever be coaxed into action. You might be able theoretically to browbeat them into getting the job done – but it won't be work you'll ever have any use for. A different approach is required.

I'm so sorry to contact you; I know I must come across as deeply annoying and unreasonable. However, I'm just wondering how you might be getting on with the project. Your work is so valuable, we need you more perhaps than you can realise. I might just be fretting, and maybe you have it all in hand, but if you could try to make sure that you can meet (ideally comfortably!) the deadline we agreed, I for one will feel so much more at ease. Needless to say, I'm simply so grateful – and deeply look forward to hearing from you whenever time allows.

The strategy and vocabulary originate in a place that doesn't immediately seem to have any connection to the modern office: international diplomacy. Diplomacy emerged as the urgently needed alternative to the devastations of war; if you could soothe and encourage, rather than insist, it might be possible to avoid besieged cities and bodies on the field. Diplomacy turned to words like 'possibly', 'maybe' and 'perhaps' in order to create space for the free (rather than enforced) assent of the other. It used praise rather than criticism and suggestion rather than a hectoring demand. It wasn't the result of cowardice or weakness, but of a painfully learned lesson in the way in which a just cause, directly stated, can completely fail to get the desired results.

In our panic, we tend to get stern and forget what we know from the inside. We ourselves don't respond well to being badgered. Instead it's the feeling that we are loved, valued, appreciated and liked that brings out the best in our cognitive capacities and builds our motivation: we feel safe enough to explore a promising but difficult line of thought; we feel encouraged to do the absolute best we can; we get more imaginative, more perceptive and more energetic.

We're encountering the work version of a large – and maddeningly central – feature of the human condition: the correctness and legitimacy of a message doesn't immediately get the person who hears it to do the reasonable or right thing. A sarcastic demolition of an absurd idea tends to entrench those who believe it; proving by facts and logic that someone is an idiot usually does little to induce them to be wise. If a teacher is openly appalled that a pupil fails to understand something, their chances of remedying the error are massively reduced; when environmental activists make us feel hopeless, sinful and guilty, we tend to turn away and pretend there is no problem with our planet.

> *I shouldn't worry, I know, you do amazing things at this company; but if there's any way you might let me know whether the project is progressing as it should, then you'd be able to put my fears finally and fully to rest. I know that, as always, you'll be able to do such a brilliant job.*

It may feel like another frantic Thursday afternoon, but in fact you are participating in an honourable and eternal struggle: to make a difficult truth powerful and attractive in the complex mind of another person.

What awkward message would you like to tell someone at work?

....
....
....
....
....

What's the raw way of saying it?

....
....
....
....
....

What's the delicate and careful way of saying it?

....
....
....
....
....

40.
Beyond Gossip

If there is one generalisation we can hazard about humans in the workplace, it is that they are – first and foremost – tricky: they make too much of a fuss or not enough of one, they fail to listen or speak incessantly, they procrastinate or rush everything unduly, they grow unfeasibly furious or lack self-confidence; they backstab or dither, panic or daydream (to start the list).

We are often alone with the problems that this throws up. There are a great many options when our computers break down; very few when those we work with destroy our peace of mind. In desperation, we have one chief source of solace: we gossip. We find an ally somewhere in the team with whom to privately discharge our accumulated sorrow at the behaviour of our colleagues.

Three highly challenging co-workers

Write down the names of three highly challenging people you are working – or have worked – with.

1.
....
2.
....
3.
....

The problem with gossip in offices isn't that it happens, but that it isn't taken seriously enough. We gossip from pain at how difficult our colleagues are combined with a background despair at ever being able to do anything more positive to alter dynamics – other than point to the problem ironically and sigh darkly over a drink in a cafe around the corner from the office. Gossip is at present a defeatist move; it doesn't hold out any hope for a more mature solution to our distress or a proper improvement in our workplace relationships.

But gossip is a lot more interesting and important than is generally understood. It holds enormously significant information about what is wrong inside a company and what could, with a few interventions, be put right. In its vague and elusive way, gossip is circling essential topics. What we gossip about are the central themes of office psychology: we're indirectly talking about communication, trust, self-worth, empathy, self-knowledge, respect, creativity and eloquence. We may not use these terms exactly, we may be sticking – in our stories – to specific people and devastating and witty takedowns of their foibles, but we are at heart pointing to multiple failures in the arena of emotional development. It is never so hard, once one starts, to focus in on the psychological issues vibrating beneath the targets of gossip, to move from caustic descriptions of a few maddening people to the identification of a range of essential (and more universal) themes of emotional existence.

From gossip to psychological investigation

Three highly challenging co-workers	What they do	Tricky psychological trait
1. Aditya	Tell marketing one thing, accounts another	People-pleasing
2. Mary-Jane	Furious with Dave's report on the meeting they organised	Defensiveness
3. Pablo	Inexplicably furious response to being left off an all-staff email by error	Paranoia

Now fill in your version ↗

1. Highly challenging co-worker

....

What they do

....

....

....

Tricky psychological trait

....

....

....

2. Highly challenging co-worker

....

What they do

....

....

....

Tricky psychological trait

....

....

....

3. Highly challenging co-worker

....

What they do

....

....

....

Tricky psychological trait

....

....

....

All of us are, to a greater or lesser extent, filled with emotional blocks, unhelpful impulses, damaging patterns of response and self-destructive urges. We are, put another way, and without anything pejorative being meant by this at all (given that everyone on the planet is like this), *immature*.

Somewhere in childhood, our trajectory towards emotional maturity will have been impeded. Even if we were sensitively cared for and lovingly handled, we can be counted upon not to have passed through our young years without sustaining a great many habits of mind that make us less than perfectly lucid, balanced and easy to interact with.

At the start of life, we are all – unavoidably – emotionally primitive: we divide people into goodies and baddies and miss the grey entirely, we scream or sulk rather than share our thoughts with a mixture of self-control and confidence. We get enraged when things don't go exactly to plan and fail to realise the impact of our words on others. We don't have much of an idea of the complexity and reality of the lives of those around us. If things go wrong, it's always someone else's fault. If we are not loved properly, we don't have a robust sense of self and are likely to lack confidence and a faith that things can eventually be OK.

Maturity looks very different: in this zone, people and things are rarely ever simply good or bad. We're ready to take responsibility; we're highly focused on communication. We resist rage or cynicism. We're diplomatic and highly aware of our capacity to wound others. We face the normal adversities of existence with a degree of security; we're not uprooted by every misfortune; we can cope if someone doesn't much like us or disagrees deeply with an idea that's important to us; we can put up with being side-lined on occasion and not always being the centre of attention.

The following table shows some of the characteristics of immaturity and, on the other hand, of maturity. In order to become mature, we need to move away from the traits and behaviours on the left and towards those on the right.

From immaturity to maturity

Immaturity	Maturity
Sulking	Explanation
Defensiveness	Learning
Refusal to teach	Becoming a good teacher
Always others' fault	Partial responsibility
People-pleasing	Social courage
Paranoia/self-hatred	Acceptance of random accident/self-love
Panic	Serenity/calm
Rigid negativity	Flexible hope
Stiffness, fear of others	Charm, ease
Procrastination	Unfrightened acceptance of tasks
Cynicism	Love
Frankness	Diplomacy

We are – all of us – stuck somewhere on the path between immaturity and its opposite, with varied progress in different subjects. We may have an emotional age of 5 in relation to communication, but of 75 in relation to empathy or self-control. We may be highly advanced in the arena of generosity but lagging badly when it comes to serenity. We may be in the top set for love but the bottom set for hope.

The reasons for our blocks and warps come down to events in childhood. A child who was frightened of a loud, domineering parent may grow up into someone who remains internally very much on the defensive, lacking confidence and worrying unduly about upsetting others. Or someone with a parent who didn't listen to them properly may end up feeling that they need always to be very blunt or assertive if they are ever to get anyone's attention. The patterns are various, but the common thread is that something that was difficult in an individual's upbringing continues to make itself felt in their grown-up working life. This is the essential story of psychotherapy – which seeks to help people by guiding them to understand the intimate history behind the troubles of their adult existence.

Maddeningly for our desire to be simple and 'professional', ordinary troubles in our early years can lead to very tricky behaviour at work.

When this goes wrong in childhood …	… this dynamic might show up at the office
A depressed but loving parent	Reluctance to pass on difficult news: an urge to people please
Alcoholic caregivers mired in self-pity	Tendency to focus on fanciful future hopes rather than realistic present plans: a dreamer
A parent's career went very badly at a key stage	Hugely cautious and negative, given to pointing out why any suggestion won't work: cynic and naysayer
A caregiver was often very busy and distracted	Always talking at meetings, starving for praise: peacock
An irritable parent who frequently lost their temper – and criticised the child unfairly	A perfectionist who won't admit to mistakes: manically defensive
Daunting parents who never allowed the child to feel at home in their own skin	A lack of charm; a stiffness of manner; unnatural and inauthentic

The list of problems and their origins is humbling in its potential length. But the strength of the connections between present behaviour and past experience has a redemptive and humane side, for the more we can understand of what drives our actions and feelings, the more we can explain and forgive and be forgiven. We can move from being merely thought weird or cruel to being conceived of in richer and kinder terms.

In an emotionally literate office, it will be broadly accepted that everyone in a team is going to bring certain immaturities into their working lives. No-one was perfectly parented and so everyone bears (more or less openly) a range of inner wounds that will affect their attitudes and behaviours. Knowing this and being able to discuss it with sympathetic insight invites a vital degree of psychological wisdom where there might otherwise only have been loneliness, irritation or impatience.

Until more or less now, it never seemed obvious that thinking about people's early histories could have anything very much to do with running a business or working in an office. It still feels odd. But the rationale is direct: to operate a complex modern organisation well, we need to get on with one another, but we won't be able to do so properly until we can find a language to identify and define our psychological immaturities (without embarrassment or shame) and are then able to address them collectively in a supportive and open-minded atmosphere. This is what it will mean to build emotionally intelligent offices.

41.
Think Strategically

There's a fundamental distinction to be made between two kinds of thinking: figuring out what we would like to achieve and working out how to achieve it. Or, put another way, there's a key difference between *strategy* on the one hand and *execution* on the other. Strategy is about determining our overall aims, and execution comprises everything that follows once we've decided: the practical activities required to put our plans into action.

It's natural to assume that we would all instinctively spend a lot of time on strategy before we ever turned our attention to execution – given that, however successful we might be in carrying out our plans, what really counts is having the right plans to work from in the first place. Our results can only ever be as good as the aims that first led to them.

But there's a paradoxical aspect to the way our minds operate: as a general rule, we're a great deal better at execution than at strategy. We appear to have an innate energy for working through obstacles to our goals and an equally innate resistance to pausing to understand what these goals should rightly be. We seem to be as lackadaisical about strategy as we are assiduous about execution.

We see the outcome of this bias across many areas. We concentrate far more on making money than on figuring out how to spend it optimally. We put a lot more effort into becoming 'successful' than into assessing how dominant notions of success could make us content. At a collective level, corporations are a great deal more committed to the efficient delivery of their existing products and services than on stepping back and asking afresh what the company might truly be trying to do for their customers. Nations are more devoted to growing their GDP than to probing at the benefits of increased purchasing power. Humanity is vastly better at engineering than philosophy: our planes are a good deal more impressive than our notions of what we should travel for; our abilities to communicate definitively outstrip our ideas of how to understand one another.

In every case, we prefer to zero in on the mechanics, on the means and the tools rather than on the guiding question of ends. We are almost allergic to the large first-order enquiries: what are we ultimately trying to do here?

What would best serve our happiness? Why should we bother? How is this aligned with real value?

There are tragic consequences to this over-devotion to execution. We rush frantically to fulfil hastily chosen ends, we exhaust ourselves blindly in the name of sketchy goals, we chain ourselves to schedules, timelines and performance targets – but all the while, we avoid asking what we might really need in order to flourish and so frequently learn, at the end of a lifetime of superhuman effort, that we had the wrong destinations from the start.

Perhaps it should not surprise us that our minds have such a pronounced bias towards executive labour over strategic reflection. From an evolutionary perspective, mulling over strategic questions was never a high priority. For most of history, the strategic goals would have been patently obvious: to find sufficient things to eat, to reproduce, to get through the winter and to keep the tribe safe from attack. Execution was where all the urgent and genuine difficulties lay: how to light a fire in wet weather, how to make sharper arrowheads, where to find wild strawberries or the right leaves to calm down an inflammation. We are the descendants of generations that made a succession of complex discoveries in the service of a few basic goals. Only in the conditions of modernity – where we are surrounded by acute choices as to what to do with our lives and when our aim is happiness rather than sheer survival – have strategic questions become at once necessary and very costly to avoid.

Little about our formal education has prepared us for this development. At school, 'working hard' still means dutifully following the curriculum, not wondering whether or not it happens to be correct. 'Why should we study this subject?' sounds, to most teachers, like an insult and a provocation, rather than the birth of an admirably speculative mindset. Once we start employment, most companies want the bulk of their employees to execute orders rather than reflect on their validity. We might be reaching middle age before we are granted the first formal incentives to think strategically.

Even in daily life, raising strategic questions can feel tiresome and odd. To ask, 'What's the point of doing this?' is easy to mistake for a piece of provocative negativity. If we challenge our acquaintances with any degree of seriousness with, 'What is a good holiday?' or 'What is a relationship for?', 'What is a satisfying conversation?' or 'Why do we want money?', we risk coming across as absurd and pretentious – as though such large questions were by definition unanswerable.

They tend not to be, and the dangers lie in never daring to raise them with enough vigour at the outset. We already possess a great deal of fragmentary, disorganised but important information that could help us to make progress with the larger strategic dilemmas. We have already been on a sufficient number of holidays and shopping trips, we have already had some relationships and been through a number of career shifts, we have had a chance to observe the connections between what we do and how we feel – and so we have, at least in theory, gathered the necessary material from which to draw rich conclusions as to our happiness and our purpose, as to meaning and the right human ends. We have the data; the challenge is to process it by running it through the sieve of the larger questions.

We should dare to move the emphasis of our thinking away from execution and towards strategy.

Mental manoeuvre

1. An immediate step is to grow more conscious of the way we are presently spending our time: we might be devoting 95% of our waking hours to execution and a mere 5% to strategy. Acknowledging the unfair bias, we should strive to ensure that at least 20% of our efforts are henceforth devoted to reflecting on the deeper 'why' questions, before we allow ourselves to 'relax' into the more familiar and routine work of execution.

2. We should observe how often and how naturally we devote our time to executing our ideas before we have submitted them to adequate scrutiny. We should note our discomfort around questions like: why is this a worthwhile effort? Where will I really be in a few years if this goes right? How is this connected up with what fulfils me? What is the point here? And we should watch our comparative enthusiasm for launching ourselves into projects in a hurry, for fretting only about the lower-level procedural hiccups and for ensuring that we are too 'busy' ever to leave time for reflection. We should grow suspicious of our covert devotion to rushing over enquiry.

3. We need, to accompany us in this, to redraw where prestige is accorded, to downgrade the glamour that presently clings to frantic busyness and to raise, to a corresponding degree, the image of speculative reflection.

We need a new, collective sense of what truly hard work might involve – and even what it might look like. It won't necessarily be the person who runs from meeting to meeting or juggles international phone calls who is genuinely engaged in working hard; it might be the person sitting at the window, gazing out at the clouds, occasionally cupping their head in their hands and writing something down in a little notebook.

4. We need support with how uncomfortable strategic thinking can feel. We need to be reassured that we aren't unusually wicked or flighty to be tempted to act rather than think – and should forgive ourselves for the strength of our wish to avoid all large, first-order questions. We need encouragement to stick at probing the point and the meaning, even when the overwhelming desire is to bury ourselves in correspondence or scan the news. We need to notice how oddly and humblingly lazy we (all) are where it really counts.

Consider the difference between a supplier that will sell you more or less whatever you happen to want vs the ideal-fantasy advisor who tries to hone and refine your choices. It's the difference between, for instance, a department store and the perfect style consultant.

If you could employ (free of charge) such a person, what might they say to you?

....

....

....

....

....

How much of your mental energy do you really give to grappling with promoting your long-term needs and interests? (Be sure to distinguish anxiety from careful thinking.)

....

....

....

....

Imagine a very benign and intelligent committee tasked with defining where you should be in five or ten years' time. What might they be discussing? What might their report look like?

....

....

....

....

42.
Learn to Be 'Lazy'

At times, perhaps without quite knowing why, we slip into a resolutely 'lazy' mood. We're simply not able to write anything new, or we can't face setting up any more meetings. We don't want to clean the fridge or go out to befriend prospective clients. All we have an appetite for, it seems, is to loll on the sofa and maybe dip randomly into a book, wander down to the shops and buy a packet of biscuits, or spend an hour or so soaking in the bath. We might, at an extreme, merely want to sit by the window and stare at the clouds. For a long time.

In such states of mind, we're liable to be rapidly stigmatised as profoundly (and incorrigibly) 'lazy' by friends or – more painfully – by our own conscience. Laziness feels like a sin against the bustling activity of modernity; it seems to bar us from living successfully or from thinking well of ourselves in any way. But to consider the matter from another perspective, it might be that at points the real threat to our happiness and self-development lies not in our failure to be busy, but in the very opposite scenario: in our inability to be 'lazy' enough.

Outwardly idling does not have to mean that we are neglecting to be fruitful. It may look to the world as if we are accomplishing nothing at all, but below the surface a lot may be going on that's both important and, in its own way, very arduous. When we're busy with routines and administration, we're focused on the elements that sit at the front of our minds: we're executing plans rather than reflecting on their value and ultimate purpose. But it is to the deeper, less accessible zones of our inner lives that we have to turn in order to understand the foundations of our problems and arrive at decisions and conclusions that can govern our overall path. Yet these only emerge – shyly and tentatively – when we are feeling brave enough to distance ourselves from immediate demands, when we can stare at clouds and do so-called nothing at all.

We need to distinguish between emotional and practical hard work. Someone who looks extremely active, whose diary is filled from morning until night, who is always running to answer messages and meet clients may appear the opposite of lazy. But secretly, there may be a lot of avoidance going on beneath the outward frenzy. Busy people evade a different order of undertaking. They are practically a hive of activity, yet they don't get round to working out their real feelings about their work. They constantly delay the investigation of their own direction. They are lazy when it comes to understanding particular emotions about a partner or friend. They go to every conference but don't get around to thinking about what their status means to them. They catch up regularly with colleagues but don't consider what the point of money might be. Their busyness is a subtle but powerful form of distraction.

Our lives might be a lot more balanced if we learnt to reallocate prestige, pulling it away from those with a full diary and towards those wise enough to allow for long afternoons of reflection. We should think that there is courage not just in travelling the world, but also in daring to sit at home with one's thoughts for a while, risking encounters with certain anxiety-inducing or melancholy, but also highly necessary, ideas. Without the shield of busyness, we might bump into the realisation that our relationship has reached an impasse, that our work no longer answers to any higher purpose or that we feel furious with a family member who is subtly exploiting our patience. The heroically hard worker isn't necessarily the one in the business lounge of the international airport; it might be the person daydreaming in a café or doodling on a pad of paper.

The point of 'doing nothing' is to clean up our inner lives. There is so much that happens to us every day, so many excitements, regrets, suggestions and emotions that we should – if we are living consciously – spend at least an hour a day processing. Most of us manage, at best, a few minutes – and thereby let the marrow of life escape us. We do so not because we are forgetful or bad, but because our societies protect us from our responsibilities to ourselves through their cult of activity. We are granted every excuse not to undertake the truly difficult labour of leading more conscious, searching and intensely felt lives.

The next time we feel extremely lazy, we should imagine that perhaps a deep part of us is preparing to give birth to a big thought. As with a pregnancy, there is no point hurrying the process. We need to lie still and let the idea gestate – sure in the knowledge that it may eventually prove its worth. We may need to risk being accused of gross laziness in order one day to put in motion projects and initiatives we can feel proud of.

Timetable for emotional and practical hard work

Colour in periods of the week when you are working hard in a procedural, non-thinking way.

Colour in periods of the week when you have time to think.

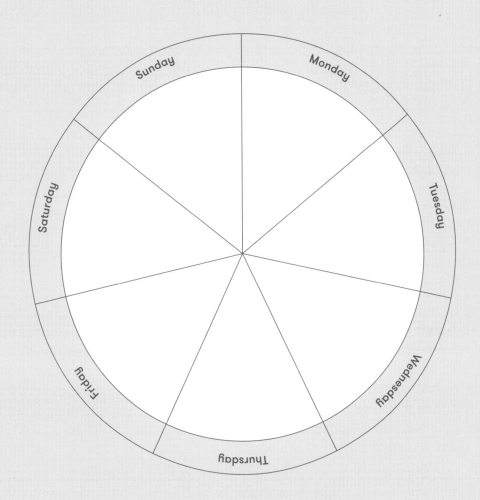

Imagine reversing the two ...

43.
You Could Leave School

Technically, most of us leave school at 18 – an event that tends to be vividly etched in memory and surrounded by considerable ceremony and emotion. And yet, rather oddly, despite appearances, many of us in fact don't manage to leave school at that point at all. In a deep part of our minds, we may still be there, deep into adulthood – not sitting in a classroom precisely, but in terms of how our minds work, as much stuck within the confines of a school-based worldview as if we were showing up for assembly every day, generating immense and unnecessary degrees of unhappiness and compromise for ourselves in the process.

What might be some of the hallmarks of an enduring, school-like way of thinking?

1. A firm belief that those in authority know what they are doing and that one's task is to obey and jump through the hoops they set for us. A desire to please teachers and gain prizes, cups and ribbons.

2. A sense that there is an implicit curriculum out there – an externally mandated map of what one needs to do to succeed – and that a wise person must dutifully subscribe to its demands.

3. A feeling that work should – when it's going well – feel substantially irksome, dull and somewhat pointless. Schools teach us to forget, or ignore, the clues offered to us by our own boredom. They teach us dangerous degrees of patience. They subtly train us in intellectual masochism.

4. The idea that you're doing it for someone else – an audience; your teachers and your parents, and their substitutes in adult life. *Make us proud. You have to shine. We've given you so much.* What matters is the performance, not any inner sense of satisfaction.

5. The belief that authority is benign. They want what is good for you and they speak on behalf of your long-term interests. *Don't think you could ever know better; distrust your instincts. We'll look after you. If you follow our rules, you will thrive.*

6. A feeling that the exam (and all its successors) is fundamentally accurate. They – those who know – have worked out the ultimate test of your value. You are what you score.

7. Every school is, in addition, a miniature society – equipped with a strong sense of what values to revere and codes to follow. Bullies lurk, ready to mock and identify any departures from the norm. You can't escape them; they are next to you in class every day. They will spot and persecute the weirdos; they can ruin your life. You learn to cower and adjust your attitudes. Following the herd is paramount.

All these ways of thinking don't require us to be sitting in a geography class. We might be in an office, selling garden furniture to the Belgian market and thinking like this; we might have children of our own and by all appearances be an adult, and yet still be living inside as though there were 'exams' to pass and cups to be won.

What would it mean to break the mould? What would it mean finally to leave school? It would mean knowing some of the following:

1. There is no one way, no guaranteed set path to fulfilment laid out by authority figures. 'They' don't know. No one knows.

2. The safe path may be entirely dangerous to our flourishing.

3. Our boredom is a vital tool. It is telling us what is slowly killing us – and reminding us that time is monstrously short.

4. Authority is not, by definition, benign. The teachers and their substitutes have no real plan for you – except insofar as it suits their own advancement. It looks like they want what is good for you, but in reality they want you to play their game for their own benefit. At the end, they

will have no proper prize to offer you. They'll give you a colourful card and send you to the golf course and the grave, and you will have wasted your life.

5. It doesn't matter what the bullies think. No one is normal. You can dare to make enemies; indeed, you must do so as the price to pay for having developed a character and found something truly to believe in.

We can detect, and help, our secret schoolchild by asking certain questions …

What were you like at school? Did you try to fit in, or did you fit in without realising you were trying?

....

....

....

Did you ever feel bullied? What did the bullies fail to recognise in you?

....

....

....

To what extent do you instinctively side with the powers that be over the rebels? (Which is not to suggest that there aren't many very absurd ways of being rebellious.)

....

....

....

When do you feel bored at work? If tasks were tweaked in some ways, would that reduce your frustration? How might those changes help those you are working for?

....

....

....

We shouldn't be tough on ourselves for lingering so long. School is an immensely impressive system; we start there when we are not much bigger than a chair. For more than a decade, it's all we know, it is the outside world – and it is what those who love us most tell us we should respect. It speaks with immense authority not just about itself, but about life in general. It is sold to us as a preparation for the whole of existence. But, of course, the main thing it does is prepare us for yet more school; it is an education in how to thrive within its own profoundly peculiar rules – with only a tenuous connection to the world beyond.

Knowing all this, we might do a very strange-sounding thing: finally work up the courage to leave our inner school – be it at 28, 35 or 62 – and enter the wider, boundless world we have been in flight from for too long.

44.
Entrepreneurship

Starting one's own business is one of the most creative, meaningful and practically sensible things one could ever do with one's life, yet few of us ever get close to giving it a go. Some of the obstacles are technical and economic, but many others are squarely in the psychological realm. They're the sort of problems aspiring business owners should rightly turn to psychotherapy and philosophy for help with.

The first of these is the confidence-destroying, background suspicion that if an idea for a business is genuinely any good, someone must have had it already. This melancholy thesis tells us that capitalism is hugely over-developed as it is: we have all the businesses we need and therefore there can be nothing left for a new entrant profitably to do.

But to see how wrong this is, we need only ask ourselves if we are continuously content in every area of our lives.

This is because business can be defined as the organised attempt by one group of people to solve another's problems. In which case, business will only ever be mature when every last human has reached a state of total satiety. Whenever we spot a problem – in our own lives or those of others – we are also spotting, at least in theory, a latent business waiting to be developed. The only true end point for capitalist effort (and time for legitimate unemployment) is the conclusion to all our problems.

One way to think about what businesses the world still needs is to run through an average day and ask oneself where one can spot, in any domain, problems, shortfalls, frictions or inefficiencies. There are, of course, a few areas where capitalism is so well developed that there really seem to be no problems at all. One is unlikely to have anything to complain about around the number of breakfast cereals there are to buy or the number of options one has when picking a pencil. As economists put it, certain markets are truly mature already.

But in many other domains, untreated problems – large and small – assail us from every direction. We face a multitude of situations where we'd ideally like a solution and none seem to exist, at least not in a form or at a price that suits. We've had a furious argument with our partner and there's no one to help; the view from the window is dispiritingly ugly; we're lacking interesting friends; there aren't any Italian restaurants that pay attention to calories; we feel we're not making the most of our opportunities; the media we consume titillates but doesn't nourish us. In a daunting number of domains, we have problems large and small – and no one seemingly interested in fixing them. That's at once an inconvenience and welcome proof of how extraordinarily undeveloped our economies still are.

Often missed here is the distinction between technical and psychological innovation. Too frequently, we imagine that enterprise can only expand when people make a technological breakthrough, when a new gadget or motor or medicine is brought to market. But this is to underestimate the enormous possibilities that stem from what one can term 'psychological innovation' – in other words, when businesses are founded that solve problems not because they have a new bit of machinery, but because they have evolved new insights, psychological in nature, into the problems of other people.

The culture of business naturally encourages the new entrepreneur to do market research, but this typically fails because most of the world's good ideas could not have been described by an audience ahead of their creation, and therefore registered on a marketer's questionnaire.

The biggest source of insight into the sorts of problems around which a good business can be built is the individual. It is from close observation of the problems one has personally encountered, and minded encountering, that a robust business has a chance to emerge. The best way to understand the needs of millions of potential customers is to understand one's own needs first and foremost. The smartest form of market research is introspection.

It follows that a big reason why businesses go bankrupt is that they have failed to identify – with sufficient acuity – real problems that real people actually have, at least on a scale necessary to support an enterprise. Economic failure is in essence a failure to know other people – a failure of psychology – far more than it is a problem of execution.

Another hurdle is more personal. To be a successful entrepreneur requires us to have a focused sense of what problems we are really most interested in solving for others and ourselves. It is not enough to operate with a vague sense that, for example, we want to be creative or of use to others. Many problems may mildly intrigue us, while not concerning us enough to lend us the concentration and energy required for a decades-long assault on a topic.

Few of these psychological dimensions to business are ever handled in business education as we currently understand it. Business schools give us financial and management skills; they rarely help us with the tough psychological dilemmas.

We're trying to refocus our thoughts away from what's already been done, towards the open field of what still needs to be addressed.

What important problems do other people still have?

Where have I noticed problems in my life that are of relevance to others?

What problems do I really care about solving for others?

Business is – potentially, at least – a hugely dignified and creative field in which we solve each other's problems and make a little profit along the way. That human beings are still so deeply dissatisfied is both a social tragedy and an ongoing provocation and inspiration to anyone longing to develop their entrepreneurial capacities.

45.
Changing the World: Be Utopian!

To be accused of 'utopian thinking' is a particular insult in our times. We pride ourselves on being grounded, realistic and sober.

Insofar as we dare to imagine the future, we do so with one peculiar tic: we cautiously ask ourselves what the future will be like on the basis of current trends; we almost never ask the one big philosophically minded question: what *should* the future be like? We proceed as humble futurologists, viewing the future as something to be guessed at, rather than as bolder and more directive philosophers, committed to laying down a blueprint for the future.

To think in a utopian way is a prime political act. It involves a refusal to be limited by our current obsession with the here and now in order to focus on the world as it could and should be in order to maximise human flourishing.

The most famous utopia ever produced in the West was Plato's *Republic*, written in Athens around 380 BCE. The work lays out how the ideal society of the future should be arranged: with definitions of the ideal system of child-rearing, diet, education, law and government. This tradition of utopian writing deserves a renaissance.

In our day, much utopian thinking has gone into science fiction writing. This is one of the least prestigious of the literary arts, frequently dismissed as a subgenre consumed primarily by young men obsessed by the goriest or oddest possibilities for the future of our species. Yet science fiction is an underestimated tool in political theory and in business, for in its utopian, as opposed to dystopian, versions, it invites us imaginatively to explore what we want the future to be like – a little ahead of our practical abilities to mould it as we would wish.

Science fiction may not contain precise answers (how actually to make a jetpack or a robot that loves us) but it encourages us in something that is logically prior to, and in its own way as important as, technological mastery: the identification of a particular issue that we would like to see solved. Changes in society seldom begin with actual inventions. They begin with acts of the imagination, with a sharpened sense of a *need* for something new, be this for an engine, a piece of legislation, an idea of how people should marry or a social movement. The details of change may eventually get worked out in laboratories, committee rooms and parliaments, but the crystallisation of the wish for change takes place at a prior stage, in the imaginations of people who know how to envisage what doesn't yet exist.

In *Twenty Thousand Leagues under the Sea*, published in Paris in 1870, Jules Verne narrated the adventures of the *Nautilus*, a large submarine that tours the world's oceans, often at great depth (the 20,000 leagues – about 80,000 kilometres – refer to the distance travelled). When writing the story, Verne didn't worry too much about solving every technical issue involved with undersea exploration: he was intent on pinning down capacities he felt it would one day be important to have. He described the *Nautilus* as being equipped with a huge window even though he himself had no idea how to make glass that could withstand immense barometric pressures. He imagined the vessel having a machine that could make seawater potable, though the science behind desalination was extremely primitive at the time. And he described the *Nautilus* as powered by batteries – even though this technology was in its infancy.

Jules Verne wasn't an enemy of technology. He was deeply fascinated by practical problems. But in writing his novels, he held off from worrying too much about the 'how' questions. He wanted to picture the way things could be, while warding off – for a time – the many practical objections that would one day have to be addressed. He was thereby able to bring the idea of the submarine into the minds of millions while the technology slowly emerged that would allow the reality to take hold.

In his earlier story of 1865, *From the Earth to the Moon*, Verne had explored the notion of orbiting and then landing on the moon. He let himself imagine such a feat without getting embarrassed that it was entirely beyond the reach of all available technology.

Verne imagined that the United States would launch a mission to the moon from a base in southern Florida. He fantasised that the craft would be made of the lightest metal he knew (aluminium). He assigned what seemed an unspeakably large price tag to the venture, the equivalent of more than the entire GDP of France at the time – which turned out to be a very respectable guess at how much the Apollo programme would cost. It was a truly prescient imaginative description.

His vastly popular book may not directly have helped any engineer, but it did something that in the long run was perhaps equally important to the mission: it fostered an aspiration. It explains why NASA named a large crater on the far side of the moon after Verne in 1961, and the European Space Agency followed suit with the launch of the Jules Verne ATV in 2008, a rocket that travelled to the International Space Station carrying the original frontispiece of the 1872 edition of *From the Earth to the Moon* in its cargo bay.

The projectile, as pictured in an engraving from the 1872
illustrated edition of *From the Earth to the Moon*

The key question in science fiction – 'What would we want life to be like one day?' – has traditionally been focused on technology. And yet there is no reason why we would not perform equally dramatic thought-experiments in quite different fields, in relation to family life, relationships – or capitalism itself. That is the task of philosophical utopian thinking.

Asking oneself what a better version of something might be like, without direct tools for a fix to hand, can feel immature and naïve. Yet it's by formulating visions of the future that we more clearly start to define what might be wrong with what we have – and start to set the wheels of change in motion.

Through philosophical utopian experiments, we get into the habit of counteracting detrimental tendencies to inhibit our thinking around wished-for scenarios that seem (in gloomy present moments, at least) deeply unlikely. Yet such experiments are, in truth, often deeply relevant, because when we look back in history, we can see that so many machines, projects and ways of life that once appeared simply utopian have come to pass. Not least, Captain Kirk's phone from the 1960s TV series *Star Trek*.

We all have a utopian side to our brains, which we are normally careful to disguise, for fear of humiliation. Yet, our visions are what carve out the space in which later patient and real development can occur.

The School of Life is committed to utopian thinking and the envisaging of the world as it should be. Too often, we are wary about imagining alternatives:

- There is no point starting a new business (the market must be full already).
- There is no point pioneering a new approach to the arts (everything is already set in a fixed pattern).
- There is no point trying to live in a new way (it either exists or is mad).

A solution to this fixed and essentially unconfident mindset is to look back in history and see how much has already changed – and therefore, how much could yet change again.

- Once it was thought a good idea to bind women's feet to keep them very small.
- Once it was thought a good idea to keep slaves and flog them at every occasion.
- Once it was thought a good idea to send children down coal mines.

We may know things have changed. But we may still feel that they surely can't change again as radically. To redirect this low confidence about change, we might turn to some striking lines in T.S. Eliot's cycle of poems, *Four Quartets*:

So, while the light fails
On a winter's afternoon, in a secluded chapel
History is now and England

Four Quartets, T.S. Eliot, 1943

Winter afternoons, around 4 p.m., have a habit of feeling particularly resolved and established, especially in quiet English country chapels, many of which date back to the Middle Ages.

But T.S. Eliot wants to shake us from our complacency. He says: 'History is now and England.' In other words: everything that we associate with history – the impetuous daring of great people, the dramatic alterations in values, the revolutionary questioning of long-held beliefs, the upturning of the old order – is still going on, even at this very moment, in outwardly peaceful, apparently unchanging places. We don't see it – but only because we are standing far too close. The world is being made and remade at every instant. And therefore, any one of us has a theoretical chance of being an agent in history, on a big or small scale.

We shouldn't allow underconfidence to deprive the world of our contributions, especially as there's so much that badly needs to change. We should be confident, even at sunset on winter afternoons, of our power to join the stream of history – and, however modestly, change its course.

What is your biggest dream for society?

....

....

....

....

....

What is the most ambitious thing you would want to change about the world, if you knew you would eventually succeed?

....

....

....

....

....

How might you start – in a tiny way – this week?

....

....

....

....

....

Conclusion

Our career is a lifelong concern; it's absolutely not a question of, once and for all, finding the right job and sticking with it. Our capacity and needs are constantly growing, and the broader cultural and commercial landscape in which we operate is always shifting.

We are continually evolving. From one vantage point, we get a better view of other places where we might want to go; we discover new aspects of ourselves; we realise that the focus of our excitement or concern has matured. We're not merely changing, which is a coldly neutral way of describing life; we have built on who we were. We're more complex, sophisticated versions of ourselves and it's right that out ambitions and needs should expand or get redirected in step with our broader development.

Maybe we've now satisfied an earlier need; perhaps we wanted more money, got it and then realised it wasn't as basic a need as we once thought. Maybe we wanted to know what it was like to be at the core of power, and then, at some stage, we felt we knew enough. Without being mean to ourselves, we can accept that we needed to do things then that we don't need to do now.

Everyone, ultimately, is an idiot. We all, judged sternly, misdirect our efforts and mess up the story of who we should really have been. History will be brutal to us all. The heroes of today will be the villains of a future epoch. So, we need – as a basic moral requirement, an existential courtesy – an uncynical generosity towards ourselves. Work imposes upon us a beautiful but impossible reality: we are unfathomably complex individuals; we can never be understood – let alone employed – perfectly. We can't ever possibly find a match between who and what we really are and the overt, aggregated demands of the world.

We are living in a time that tells us that having a career is everything. Career success is desirable, but in the end this is not a remotely accurate assessment of a life. Lovely people have failed, monsters have made it to the top. It used to be – far away in the poetry of Dante or the art of Michelangelo – that a life could be judged on what one loved rather than what one overtly did for work. It's not that work is unimportant; it's just not the most important thing.

And, therefore, we can get it wrong. We will always be wondering if we've made the right career choices; we'll always be lamenting past decisions; we'll perhaps never be truly satisfied in any job. That is not because the job is wrong or terrible, but because of something glorious and a bit mad about the human condition: we reach for the unreachable, even if we can never attain it, and we are lovely because we try.

Image Credits

p. 16
David Attenborough, Life in The Undergrowth: Ep2: Taking to The Air, 2005. Photo: Mark Carwardine, © BBC Photo Archives

p. 17
Barbara Hepworth working in her studio, 1963. Photo: Val Wilmer / Courtesy Bowness

p. 40 [left]
Michelangelo, *The Prisoners*, 1523. Peter Horree / Alamy Stock Photo

p. 40 [right]
Michelangelo, *The Prisoners*, 1523. Peter Horree / Alamy Stock Photo

p. 42
Giotto, *Envy* from *The Seven Vices*, 1306. Fresco, 120 × 55 cm, Scrovegni Chapel, Padua, Italy. Public Domain / Wikimedia Commons

p. 50
Library in luxury home. pics721 / Shutterstock

p. 51 [top]
Top view 3D image of an environmentally friendly office space. alvarez / iStock Images

p. 51 [bottom]
Annie Spratt / Unsplash

p. 52
Vacant office #3. T_A_P / iStock Images

p. 82
Jean-Paul Sartre (1905–1980), French philosopher, novelist and dramatist, c. 1959. Granger Historical Picture Archive / Alamy Stock Photo

p. 135
Anonymous, *Portrait of Michel Eyquem de Montaigne*, 17th century. Versailles Museum, Versailles, France. Archivart / Alamy Stock Photo

p. 140
Francis Bacon, *Self-Portrait*, 1978. Private collection. Oil on canvas, 198.12 × 147.32 cm. © The Estate of Francis Bacon. All rights reserved, DACS / Artimage 2022. Photo: Prudence Cuming Associates Ltd

p. 141
Francis Bacon's 7 Reece Mews studio, London, 1998 © The Estate of Francis Bacon. All rights reserved, DACS / Artimage 2022. Photo: Perry Ogden

p. 142
Miffy, illustration Dick Bruna © copyright Mercis bv, 1979

p. 150
Lucius Annaeus Seneca, c. 4 BCE–65 CE. Cordoba, Cordoba Province, Spain. Ken Welsh / Alamy Stock Photo

p. 198
Engraving of a scene from Jules Verne's *De la terre a la lune (From the Earth to the Moon)*, 1872. duncan1890 / iStock images

The Couple's Workbook
Homework to help love last

Therapeutic exercises to help couples nurture patience, forgiveness and humour.

Love is a skill, not just an emotion – and in order for us to get good at it, we have to practise, as we would in any other area we want to shine in.

Here is a workbook containing the very best exercises that any couple can undertake to help their relationship function optimally – exercises to foster understanding, patience, forgiveness, humour and resilience in the face of the many hurdles that invariably arise when you try to live with someone else for the long term. Couples are guided to have particular conversations, analyse their feelings, explain parts of themselves to one another and undertake rituals that clear the air and help recover hope and passion. Not least, doing exercises together is – at points – simply a lot of fun.

ISBN: 978-1-912891-26-9
£18 | $24.99

The Calm Workbook
A guide to greater serenity

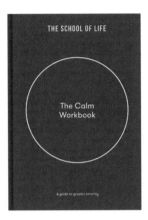

A therapeutic and consoling workbook with exercises to soothe anxiety and create a state of calm.

Most of us long to be a little calmer: too many of our days are lost to agitation and worry, stress and discord. Yet we know that we are at our best when we can manage not to panic and take challenges in our stride.

Fortunately, a calm state of mind is not a divine gift. Even those of us starting from a more agitated position can systematically understand and lay claim to it. Too many books on this subject simply explain what it would be like to be calm. This is a workbook that takes us through the practical steps required to actually become calm. It is filled with exercises and prompts that deliver the self-understanding and self-compassion on which true serenity depends. Furthermore, the book invites us to build calming routines into our daily lives.

ISBN: 978-1-912891-49-8

£18 | $24.99

The School of Life publishes a range of books on essential topics in psychological and emotional life, including relationships, parenting, friendship, careers and fulfilment. The aim is always to help us to understand ourselves better – and thereby to grow calmer, less confused and more purposeful. Discover our full range of titles, including books for children, here:

www.theschooloflife.com/books

The School of Life also offers a comprehensive therapy service, which complements, and draws upon, our published works:

www.theschooloflife.com/therapy